Is I
Cat Or !

Is My Cat OK?

How to Know...
When Your Cat Won't Say

Jeff Nichol, D.V.M.

Prentice
Hall Press

Library Of Congress Cataloging-In- Publication Data

Nichol, Jeff
   Is my cat ok? : how to know . . . when your cat won't say / Jeff Nichol.
      p.cm.
   ISBN 0-7352-0277-X
   1. Cats—Miscellanea. 2. Cats—Health—Miscellanea. 3. Cats-Diseases—
Miscellanea. 4. Cats-Wounds and injuries—Miscellanea. I. Title.

SP447.N498 2001
636.8'0887—dc21   2001021119

This book is a reference work based on research by the author. Any techniques
and suggestions are to be used at the reader's sole discretion. The opinions
expressed herein are not necessarily those of or endorsed by the publisher. The
directions stated in this book are in no way to be considered as a substitute for
consultation with a duly licensed doctor.

Printed in the United States
10 9 8 7 6 5 4 3 2 1

ISBN 0-7352-0277-X

Attention: CORPORATIONS AND SCHOOLS
Prentice Hall books are available at quantity discounts with bulk purchase
for educational, business, or sales promotional use. For information, please
write to Prentice Hall Special Sales, 240 Frisch Court, Paramus, New Jersey
07652. Please supply title of book, ISBN, quantities, how the book will be
used, date needed.

Prentice
Hall Press Paramus, NJ 07652

http://www.phdirect.com

To my caring and supportive wife, Carolyn,

who like our children and me,

loves our pets like children.

CONTENTS

Acknowledgments

This book has been a true labor of joy because of the emotion and importance that we invest in the pets who share our homes. While I have learned much about medical and behavioral needs through my formal education and professional experience, I did not reach this place alone. I have learned much from the many people and pets I encountered along the way. I have thought often about these individuals, but this is my chance to celebrate some of them. Without a team of coaches, mentors, and my own successes and failures, I would never have developed the skills to help pets and educate their loving families.

Putting all this knowledge on paper was one thing; making it readable and easy to use was quite another. Writing a weekly newspaper column and then a book has caused me to hone my writing skills, but without the help of a handful of knowledgeable and helpful folks, something of lesser value would have resulted.

In 1958 my father and I took my first dog, Scott, to an excellent veterinarian, who inspires me even still, Dr. Lyle Tuck. It was Dr. Tuck's knowledge and generous manner, and my father, Ira's encouragement, that at age 8, kicked my career into motion. A high school job as kennel boy in the employ of Dr. Howard Nurse, and the early mentoring of Dr. Bill Mullin during my time as a Boy Scout showed me what fine humans veterinarians can be. Entering veterinary school in 1970 and graduating in 1974 would have been impossible without the drive of assistant dean Dr. John Newman. Without the late "Black John," I would not be a member of the profession he so fiercely shepherded.

My days as a D.V.M. began in 1975 at the St. Francis Animal Clinic in Albuquerque, NM. Drs. Richard Heise and Dennis Elliott were my first teachers in general practice. Both of these stalwarts of the healing art of companion pets remain in practice to this day. Other doctors who have practiced under the same roof and whose daily consultation has helped me avoid mistakes and teach me good medicine and compassion are Dr. Lloyd Beal of Sacramento, CA, Dr. Virginia Vader of Nashville, TN, Dr. Sue Tornquist of Corvallis, WA, Dr. Sue Chellstorp of St. Louis, MO, and Drs. Christine Appel and Cheri Potter, who share with me now the daily ups and downs of making better the lives of canine, feline, and human animals.

Those are the people whose knowledge of veterinary medicine has made a major difference. I must also say thanks to the thousands of people who have entrusted me with the lives of their beloved pets. Without that faith, I would not have done much good. But there have been a few non-humans who have been the closest to me. These boys and girls have been my family and have stood by me through the good times and bad. They are Scott (my childhood Brittany Spaniel), Billy Bones (my beagle and first obedience dog), Bob (15 pounds of high energy, short-legged independent spirit), Frieda (the German Shepherd, who taught me patience), Juan Gomez, UD (the Airedale who, aside from being my best friend and a nationally ranked obediance competition dog, taught me fatherhood), Chase (Old English Sheepdog, the sweetest child to ever wear a dog suit), and finally the great American family dog Peter Rabbit (the Border Collie of the Nichol family who is right now teaching the next generation that being kind is better than being a barbarian).

My lifetime of cats has been no less critical to my well being and love of life. They are Polly (white-as-the-snow Persian, highly dignified), Bernard (silver Persian donated to me by a loving owner who could not afford his surgery), Arizona (the gentle orange tabby girl who died tragically beneath the wheel of a speeding car), Curious George (the Nichol boy's most special gray tabby), Pecos (the most gentle orange boy cat), and Raoul de Las Orcas (the orange tabby who is still showing no signs of aging at 15). Without this family of God's purest of spirits, my life would have been of lesser value.

Last, my gratitude goes to those who have helped make writing a skill for me. My first and greatest teacher of the English language is my mother, Joan Nichol. She is the best mom ever to grace the planet and surely the finest grammarian alive today.

What has culminated in this book began, and continues, as a weekly question/answer column for the *Albuquerque Journal*. My editors at the *Journal* who have helped my work make sense are Karen Moses (who gave me a chance to contribute in the first place), Ellen Marks, and Barb Chavez. But the first person who recognized that I had something to share in book form was Matthew Hoffman. Matthew, thanks for helping me believe I could do it.

Last, and for Prentice Hall, the publisher of the book open in front of you now, I give my thanks first to Ed Claflin whose generous wisdom and patience with a first-time author helped me stay on track and get the job done. And without the help of Mariann Hutlak, this book would not be of a quality fit to read.

A Warm Heart
for a Cold Nose

When I hear the words "pet care," it sounds too much like work—and work is something you probably don't need.

Everybody works—and most of us work way too much—so having a cat in your life shouldn't add to your workload. In fact, just the opposite. For many of us, our cats are a safe and reliable presence, a special bit of insurance against the rough times in human life. That smiling, often goofy presence is also a way to remember that maybe we're not really here just to learn hard lessons.

One mighty important reason to live on this planet is to have a great time. Pets are here not only to remind us of that, but to be our partners in having fun.

So, this won't be a book about pet care that's a lot of work. Let's make it fun and easy to allow our cats to be our partners in anything we want. They will never ask, "Are you sure you want to do that?" or "Is that the best you can do?" or "I bust my tail all day and this is the thanks I get?"

You might hear this kind of thing from other quarters in your life, but cats are a higher life form than that. No way do your pets want to be a burden on you. They just want to be there.

So here is what I'm going to do for you: I'll make it as easy as possible to keep you and your pet together for as long as possible. Yes, there's some care involved—but not work. You should all have a good time.

A special note before we get going: I use the personal pronouns "him" and "her" instead of "it" when referring to pets. My newspaper editors have often edited my columns to reflect the Queen's English. They have changed the *hims* and *hers* to *thats* and *its*. But you and I know better. We know that our pets are real individuals. They are not objects. They can't be put on a shelf when we're done playing with them. Cats have lives just like the rest of us; they are neither toys nor trophies. So I call them "him" or "her," not "it."

Interestingly, our Western culture and legal system sees pets, and all nonhuman animals, as possessions. If you've ever endured the modern American horror of divorce, you've already learned that. Back in 1988 I paid my dues to that truly life-changing cataclysmic rite of passage with the demise of my first marriage. Having finally realized that there was no way to pursue a healthy life and remain married, I was astounded to learn that pets, in the eyes of the law, have the same status as houseplants.

At that time, I had three beloved pets—Juan Gomez, an Airedale Terrier, and two orange tabby cats, Raoul and Pecos. According to the court, my former spouse and I were supposed to divide our pets like so many sets of dishes. They very well could have been a garage-sale find. I was utterly amazed that they weren't automatically going to stay alternately with each of their parents. How could it not be so? We each loved those three intensely. What a rude surprise to learn that Juan, Pecos, and Raoul were but additional items on the list of property to be divided.

The problem was solved by my former wife offering me all three in exchange for some additional cash and the return of my wedding ring. It was her final act of love for me. I jumped at the offer, coughing up both the money and the ring, and those three boys guided me into the next chapter of my life. I will remain forever indebted to my first wife. Without my dog and two cats, I could not have endured the greatest loss I have ever felt. They were, and will always be, this man's best friend. Whatever the legal system says, they are not, and will never be, potted plants.

Pets are as real as any person. Each of them has a spirit. Most of those spirits are more pure and uncluttered than ours. We have them in our lives to help us learn the real meaning of being. They are God's creatures.

Jeff Nichol, D.V.M.

Is My Cat OK?

PART 1

Coming on Board:
Why Have a Cat
in the First Place?

If you're interested enough in pets to read this book, you already have some idea of why you would invite a member of the animal kingdom (that includes you and me, by the way) to share your home. We know about companionship and nurturing; and they're good reasons. But why a different species?

There are a huge number of reasons why people have cats. Like most close personal relationships, it's kind of, well, private. So you don't need to tell me. But if you're thinking of adding a pet to your home, I recommend that you actually write down on paper why you want to do something that weird.

Weird? Sure. Just think of anyone who's been confounded by a cat's behavior that seemed so completely alien that they came to their wits' end over it. Consider that each of us has lived at least part of our lives with other people. If another person is sick, you can probably relate on some level; you might have some sense of what's going on, what to do. But a different species has some very different maladies.

If a space alien came to your home or mine and saw us with our pets, as different in appearance as they are, wouldn't they find it odd? How many nonhuman animals keep a different species as such close friends or family members in their lives? Certainly there are others with symbiotic or parasitic relationships. But these all have truly practical functions that benefit the survival of one creature or both. We pet lovers do this for very different reasons.

The veterinary profession has recognized three types of pet owners. In the first group are those of us who describe our pets as children. The second group is comprised of those who consider themselves "practical pet owners." They set limits on what they'll invest. In the third category are those who regard cats as "just animals."

If you're reading this book, I reckon you're probably the first type of pet owner. Certainly, that describes my family and me. Our household has a number of children—some just bear more of a physical resemblance to their parents than others.

By now I've been a practicing veterinarian for one half of my 50 years, and I've dealt with many pet owners. I think some of them carry secrets pretty well. Others don't. I was a very small veterinarian indeed when I got over believing that I could judge a pet owner's true motives.

The truth is, I don't have to play psychologist. My job is to help you find the right pet and make that friendship last a long time—and whatever reason you have for wanting to get involved in that relationship is strictly your business.

But it helps to get started right. Accidental pairings work out about as often as winning at roulette. I believe in attraction at first sight—but not long-term, healthy relationships at first sight. So whatever your motives for pet ownership, I will give you some guidelines for pet selection.

But what about fate, you ask? If you take a gander at a litter of kittens, doesn't the right one just run right up to you and steal your heart? Ever get married like that? Ever take a job that way? Are you crazy? Please say no.

If you want a pet and you want to get the right one, where do you start? Find yourself a veterinarian whom you can trust (you know, start a relationship). Ask for some advice on where to find a potentially healthy pet. Any D.V.M. (doctor of veterinary medicine) who's been at this very long will ask you a few useful questions, then steer you in a good direction.

This pending human–pet relationship could last a big part of your life. Take it slow and do a bit of research. This way you can make as many correct choices as possible. Much of life is a crapshoot. We'll try to minimize the gamble. Turn the page and I'll tell you more about choosing the best cat you have ever known.

PART 2

Choosing the Greatest Kitten for Your Life

Can you choose the great feline friend who will be the faithful excellent companion you have always wanted? I think you can, but there are many *ifs* involved. This is an issue both simple and complicated at once.

In my attempt to help you find the cat you want, I will also try to help you avoid the cat who could make your life a living hell (or a living heck, if the cat is only moderately evil). So let's start with expectations.

Dogs are a lot like people. Cats are not. Each year, 25 percent of pet cats leave their homes permanently. Only one-third of cats stay in the same home for their entire lives. For the average American home, dogs are much more likely to stay put. This is not because the cats were bad, but because the cat owner's choices were bad.

What Is a Cat?

Kittens seem to take after their dads. In fact, cats get most of their personalities from their dads. Sorry to say, most of these losers are nowhere to be found when the kids need their diapers changed. No kitten support, no college tuition. Mom may be quite friendly—a real charmer, but meeting her doesn't do much good. Even if she's tolerant and kindly, her children could be life-long barbarians. Sounds like my family.

But that's only the beginning. The biggest difference between cats and nearly all other mammalian species is that they are fundamentally asocial. In other words, they are natural loners.

But wait, you say. You've known lots of cats who have groomed and cared for each other. There are reasons for this that I will explain later. For now, understand that choosing a kitten is very different from choosing a human friend, or a romantic partner, or a job. These life choices are based on social needs. Cats don't really have social needs.

But the mere fact that cats are not a highly socialized species does not mean they don't have an important process of socialization. It's just not essential for their survival, the way it is for animals like humans, dogs, or any other species that live in communities (packs, cities, flocks, or herds).

If cats *don't* have lots of human handling in ample amounts at the appropriate times in early kitten-hood development, they manage to look after themselves and do fine. But these cats cannot be effectively tamed and kept as acceptable pets. What you need to find out is whether the kittens you are examining have been socialized for you.

If you arrive at the home of the proud owner of an aesthetically pleasing litter of dynamite kitties, and you learn they have not been properly acclimatized to humans, you probably want to feign acute abdominal distress and make a quick exit.

KITTEN SOCIALIZATION FACTS

During their first three weeks of life, kittens spend their non-sleeping and noneating time imprinting on their mothers. In other words, they learn how to be cats. Between ages 3 weeks and 9 weeks, their brains allow them to become accustomed to any species that shares their lives—and I do mean *any* species. You can introduce rats, mice, birds, dogs, or humans during this time, and whoever they associate with will be seen as friends throughout the lives of those kittens. But, if that window of time is missed, the result will be a cat who responds in a socially inappropriate way to other creatures.

Thus, orphaned kittens, raised without kitten companions, will have a hard time with other cats the rest of their lives. Kittens raised by feral mothers simply cannot be tamed as decent pets if they don't have human contact at the right time. On the other hand, kittens who were exposed to non-frightened rodents or dogs have no hard feelings at all for these "natural enemies."

There are cats who like people, and others who like to bite and scratch people. If a kitten was handled gently by many different humans as a youngster, he or she is likely to be a relaxed and affectionate pet. Kittens handled roughly are more prone to biting and scratching when they are petted. And, just like children, kittens go through phases with gradual transitions.

As a general rule, it's best to allow kittens to stay with their mothers and littermates until they're 5 weeks or older. Kittens who are adopted when they're younger than this can become aggressive toward other cats—or may "act out" with self-mutilation behavior like biting or chewing themselves.

So, you can determine a lot about a kitten if you just ask the owner a few simple questions, such as:

➠ When were the kittens born?

➠ Who handled them and when?

➠ How much were the kittens handled?

➠ Have the kittens learned to play roughly or gently?

➠ What was Dad like? (Aside from being an irresponsible lout, that is.)

If they were given a whole bunch of gentle affection every day, there's a good chance this litter has the kitten you're looking for.

TEMPERAMENT TESTING

Now let's pick a great kitty.

I love cats. I can tell within a few minutes of evaluating a given litter of kittens if they are a great bunch or if they are just not right. So let's say the answers to the above questions are good ones and you're standing there gazing upon a frolicking, cavorting bunch of cuties. Try not to miss some important signs.

If you are going to be effective in finding the right kitty, you'll need some quality time with the contestants. Even if you're getting a cat for the kids, leave the kids at home. And ask the cat owner to let you meet the litter alone. (Yes, somehow you need to convince the owner to leave the room.)

Then—sit quietly and observe. This is critical. The babies will tell you nearly everything you need to know if you watch and wait.

If the babies are between 5 and 10 weeks of age, they are in a social period. You'll see the kitten litter politics being played out in front of you, and it won't take long to see who is the dominant kitten. This is the pushy one who's in charge. You probably don't want this tough guy or gal—it's usually the one who's less affectionate than the others.

Is there a runt? We all feel sorry for this underdog (undercat?). But think twice about the little one. If this baby was seriously intimidated by its brethren, he or she may be poorly socialized. And please remember that you should not feel obligated to adopt the least desirable kitten because perhaps no one else will. You're only choosing for yourself; someone else may have completely different preferences and different ideas of what kind of cat they want to live with.

PICKING AND CHOOSING

After you've observed the kittens in a bunch, it's time for individual evaluations. You'll need a separate room where you can take each kitten.

Quietly pick up a kitten and let the baby sit in your hands. Is he relaxed or anxious? If the kitten is restless, he probably won't relate well in social situations.

Now put the kitten on the ground and start to walk away. Does the kitten follow? What happens when you stop? Does the kitten stay relaxed and start to explore his or her surroundings? If so, that's a good sign.

Clap your hands. Does the kitten panic and bolt? A jumpy cat is likely to remain that way—so if you want a relaxed, friendly cat, the panicky kind probably isn't for you.

Sometimes the kitten's posture can tell a lot, too. Watch for a few minutes, and you might see some clues. Here's what they mean:

Head Up. If a kitten has her head up and a straight back, she's relaxed. And if the tail is straight out, you have a cool cat. You want this.

Straight Rear Legs with a High Rump. These are the signs of a take-charge cat—the kind who will tell you where to go. This could be your new boss. Is that what you want?

Belly Up. If the kitten you are observing rolls on her back, you have a kitten who believes that he or she may be in a conflict soon. It also usually means that, in such a conflict, this cat will fight only if really pushed. He would prefer to run away. This is not a relaxed posture. I would avoid this kitty.

Arched Back. I don't think you need much help here. This cat is ready to rumble.

Purring. This may seem like an obvious sign of affection. But it's a little more subtle than that. There are actually two kinds of purrs, though you'd need to be an expert on cat-speak to tell them apart.

As we all know, many cats and kittens purr when they are content. If you are holding a prospective family member who purrs, it's understandable that you would be favorably inclined. But did you know that many kittens purr in a slightly different way when they are anxious? If being held causes anxiety, you'll want to know it.

So, how can you tell? Believe it or not, a meow is much more reliable than a purr. If the baby meows when you hold him or her, you almost certainly have a relaxed kitten.

PLAY

This could be among the most useful predictors of social success in a young kitten. While nearly all kittens play, you'll learn a lot if you take note of *who* plays *how*.

Kittens who play roughly, with claws extended, are likely to do the same with you at home. Between ages 5 and 10 weeks, their socialization period, you'll want a pet who acts, well, social. It's become clear to behaviorists that timid kittens in this age group are likely to remain aloof throughout their lives.

To be concise, if the kitten won't play with his family, he won't play with you, either. The bottom line is that if you like the way a kitten interacts with his or her siblings during this phase of development, then that baby may have your name on him.

BREED VARIATIONS

Folks who are big on a particular breed feel strongly. Many pure-breed cat fanciers feel such a gut-level commitment to their breed that they find it impossible to allow others to have opinions. I'll provide a few facts.

The cat breeds that have been popular for a long time have, in some cases, been carefully developed to make good social pets. The best example may be the Siamese. This works because, when a breed is common, there are many individuals who are not even eighteenth cousins once removed. The gene pool is big. You can mate personalities that you like and not have a case of incest on your hands.

It's a different matter when you're dealing with the less common breeds of cats. In many cases, those rarer breeds come from very small families of cats that were imported into this country— hence, a small gene pool. Interbreeding these closely related individuals has helped to perpetuate a host of physical defects. It has also had the effect of producing more asocial cats.

Thus I recommend popular breeds, or best of all, the all-American mix. Fortunately, the vast majority of cats for you to have in your life are the latter.

NOTHING BUT THE BEST

I hope reading this discourse on the nuts and bolts of kitten behavior has been helpful and not a chore. For many cat lovers, the addition of a new kitty is such an affair of the heart that it seems painful to even introduce things like logic.

All of us feline-friendly folk are fools for a fuzzy face. But despite the urge to open our hearts to every deserving cat, I advocate using our heads, too. Carefully select the greatest companion of your life.

Life is short and friendships are precious. Wonderful cats are that way because they are well matched to their human counterparts. But to build that relationship into everything you want it to be, you must start with a good match.

PART 3

Dr. Nichols' Cardinal Rules of Cat Care

Rules for cat care?

You must think I'm joking.

The word *rules* implies structure, and who ever heard of a cat with any regard for structure?

Cats don't care about that stuff. We humans (most of us anyway) believe in some semblance of organization. We may not like all of the laws that govern our lives, but we seem to agree that they're somehow necessary.

But cats . . . well, they are a little different. To them, any rules are for beings from other planets, not for them. In fact they think *people* are from another planet. But, heck, we do have a few good points. So our cats hang out at our house and we think they're cool. So cool, in fact, that people like us can't imagine life without them.

We interact with them, feed and care for them, and generally treat them like our children. Pet people need that. And it's mighty healthy too. Folks with pets have been shown to live longer, healthier, better lives.

We recognize the differences between us and our cats and we like it that way. But cats are different not because they're smarter than we are nor that they're smarter than dogs, either. It's because they are a different species of animal than humans. Not only do they have some very different behaviors and methods of communication; they are fundamentally different socially. That's basic.

Humans, like most other mammalian species, are community animals. Most people live in cities, horses in herds, birds in flocks. Cats, by contrast, are loners. Heresy, you say? We all know folks whose group of cats seems to do just fine together.

But while they can commune cooperatively, there is an element of stress in a group of cats. It is not their natural state. When a member of a more highly socialized species, like a dog, becomes ill, others in the community come to his or her aid. These critters communicate their need for help. But cats, being natural loners, say nothing. The typical sick or injured cat crawls into a secluded space and does his or her best to get well alone. So if you love your cat, you must learn to observe his or her behavior carefully.

But as much as we understand why we share our lives with cats, we still may have a hard time. What does it mean when a cat vomits often, or frequently urinates in the wrong place? How can you effectively discipline cats—or at least change their behavior?

Some cats are a breeze to live with. Others can make you crazy. My job in presenting the information in this book is to make a lot of this easier. I'll help you sort through the problems and solve a few of them, too.

THE BEGINNING OF FELINE GUIDANCE

In addition to fixing a flock of feline physical frailties in a general veterinary practice, I have training and broad experience in the management of their behavioral problems as well. But before we try to correct bad behavior, we must first know and understand what is normal.

What is normal for a cat? Is it reasonable to believe that what is normal in a human home is somehow typical in the wild, too?

There are perfectly happy, well-functioning wild cats who belong to the same species as that cuddly kitty who's rubbing your leg right now. How can those two sides of a cat be compatible? On one hand, there's the independence of the hunting feline survivalist; on the other hand, the close companionship of a housecat.

While our cats are a truly adaptable species, they are the same creatures in the wild as they are at home. It isn't that they adapt to fit our lives. Instead, we are seeing different sides of the same coin. Within the confines of our homes, we bring out one side of a cat while life in the wild accentuates a whole different part of the beast.

To manage this complex web of intricate contradictions, I offer you my Cardinal Rules of Cat Ownership. I'm sure they don't cover everything, but I think they hit the high points.

Dr. Jeff's Cardinal Rules of Cat Ownership

RULE 1. A cat who doesn't come when called may just be stuck up. But cats instinctively hide serious illness. So the cat who hides may be gravely ill.

Stuck up? Well, of course your cat is stuck up. All cats are, to some degree.

But a sick cat isn't acting. Don't interpret a cat's behavior using human rules.

RULE 2. Any cat who spends too much time in the litter pan needs a doctor fast. His plumbing can kill him.

The inability to pass urine or stool is a miserable state. But it can be a lot more than that. Our cats, being private, don't advertise their constipation or inability to urinate unless they're in real trouble. Constipation is common in older cats. As in humans, it usually develops gradually. It is important and it's treatable, but it's not an emergency. Only cats who are in excruciating pain will cry out. So, again, you must be observant.

If a cat makes frequent visits to the litter pan, you might assume that the problem is constipation; your job, however, is to assume nothing. Take a close look at what, if anything, your cat leaves behind when he walks away. To know for sure what all the squatting is about, dump the litter and put a piece of clean white paper in the bottom of the pan. Add a small to moderate amount of litter, then check the paper after the next visit. Look for small amounts of blood-tinged fluid on the white paper.

If the problem child is a male cat, have a helper hold the kitty's front end. Reach up to your cat's abdomen from between his rear legs and gently squeeze. If that boy cries, go to the nearest veterinary hospital. That little guy may have a urinary blockage. Kidney shut down could be just around the corner.

Move quickly. If he doesn't get help fast, he may die.

RULE 3. Cats who cough or breathe too fast are in trouble now.

Here is another big difference in *Felis silvestris catus* (that's fancy-speak for domestic cat). Most other species cough every now and then. Even if it's due to a respiratory or heart problem, it may not be an emergency. Coughing, in many creatures, may even resolve on its own.

Not in cats. In another demonstration of their rugged individualism, cats are loath to make an outward show of a disability. If they have any breathing impairment, they simply adjust their lives so that they require less breathing. In other words, they do more sitting still and less running around.

Now, that subtle change in behavior can be tough to observe. Most of the time when I look at my cat, he's just kicking back anyway. If I don't require him to run around, I won't know whether he can. Only when lung disease gets really advanced does a cat's breathing get difficult and rapid, even when he's at rest. A cat with a slow accumulation of lung fluid just doesn't jump around to chase mice and dust bunnies.

If your first clue is your cat's rough breathing while she's sitting still, well, she's already in deep trouble. Make that baby's trip to the doctor stress-free, but get there fast.

RULE 4. Eighty-five percent of all skin lumps and bumps on cats are malignant. Have them removed soon.

Everybody who wants surgery for their cat, stand up and wave.

Hmm, no takers?

Well, I'm not surprised. I haven't met many people who favor getting their cat cut open. Most of us will postpone, delay, rationalize, or deny that our cat has any problem requiring surgery until a skin mass begins to ooze and stink. We'd rather shrug and say, "Oh, it doesn't seem to be growing—much." Or "He's getting a bit older. It's normal to get lumps and bumps when somebody ages."

Well, don't shrug.

Nowadays we are informed consumers. If we don't feel comfortable with professional advice, we'll get a second opinion. I give second opinions all the time, right after my first opinion and just before my third opinion—all to the same pet owner. Cats who have lumps and bumps of the skin—what are called "skin masses"—are usually terminal if those skin masses are ignored. That's why my first, second, and third opinions are all the same: When in doubt, cut it out.

I've seen the studies, and I've treated cancer in cats since 1974. There are times to be conservative, but not when your cat has skin cancer. Sure, you can hope that it's a benign skin mass, but betting on that is a long shot.

All competent veterinarians remove all feline skin masses with "wide, deep, aggressive excisions." In other words, we take a lot of seemingly normal tissue around the mass and beneath it. We know that if we cut across the advancing microscopic tumor cells, we rile them up—and they're not cute when they're mad. They advance much faster. If your veterinarian advises you to "just keep an eye on your cat's skin tumor to see if it grows," pay your bill and leave.

RULE 5. Cats who won't eat may be finicky. They may also be sick. Not eating is often the first real sign of serious illness.

This is a tough call. Even the most devoted and knowledgeable cat owners get fooled. Some are so concerned if their cat fails to eat every time that they have an ever-ready smorgasbord of gastronomic delights waiting constantly in the wings of their kitchens. Let's not get carried away. The central concern is not that a cat will wither away and blow off in a stiff breeze if one meal is missed. The point is, if a consistent eater stops eating consistently, there may be cause for closer observation.

The hard part is that all cats are different. A lot of cats have variable appetites one day to the next normally. So I suggest two approaches.

Number One: Don't vary your cat's diet. Oh, I know, they like variety just like you and I—and eating is life's greatest pleasure, isn't it? It better not be. You got that cat for fun and mutual enjoyment—you know, a relationship. What kind of relationship do we have if the best part is you training the cat to become a feline garbage disposal and the cat training you to deliver a multitude of diverse menu items at his whim? I think not.

Feed the same high-quality hard, dry diet (moistened with water for indoor males) twice daily in measured amounts. Your job is to protect the health and well being of that trusting friend. Feed no junk. Control that kitty's diet to maintain a healthy weight. (Your veterinarian should advise you on your cat's ideal weight.)

Number Two: If your cat's intake changes, go into vigilance mode. Still normally active? Normal bowel movements and urine output? Drinking a normal amount? Less? More? Showing signs of weakness or lameness? Cries when handled? Call the doctor. Invest in an exam fee and be sure, but please, eat the caviar yourself. It tastes sooo good. I love my cat, but I don't share the champagne either.

RULE 6. Cats who do bad things, like urinating on your bed, are quite naughty—but you can't train them. You can fix the problem, but you'll have to do all the work.

You have to wonder.

We humans communicate by speaking words; writing notes; sending e-mail, voice mail, hate mail, junk mail, and chain letters.

We've used carrier pigeons and smoke signals. But cats do none of that. They do something like peeing on your bed.

Or worse.

I know one cat who somehow crapped under the pillow of his college fraternity owner repeatedly. Maybe the cat disliked Dad's girlfriend. Maybe he wanted to move to another frat house or thought his owner should change his major. Who knows? Annoying, isn't it?

But losing one's patience doesn't help. In most cases, getting rid of your cat won't help either—because you'll miss that cat.

One more thing: The greatest cause of death in cats is neither a disease nor an injury. It's euthanasia—and the most common reason for euthanasia is behavior problems. You may not be the person ordering the death of your cat, but if his behavior is unacceptable and you move him out of your home, his behavior is likely to restart in his next abode. His ultimate destination may be animal control.

The solutions to problems like this are not simple, but they work. Nearly every behavior problem cat can work out. Read the sections of this book on feline behavior problems. I cover all of the common ones. And, yes, you will do all the work. I'm sorry. Life isn't fair. You already knew that. Now you know that I know it, too.

■ ■

RULE 7. Cats who vomit more than twice in one day need help fast. Cats who vomit now and then need help at the next available appointment.

Puking pussycats. Hey, I never promised you rose gardens in this tome on cat health. It's all here, the good, the bad, and the vomit.

That said, I really hate it when people call or e-mail me and ask why their cat is vomiting. If I were to list every possible cause of vomiting in cats, you'd be holding a much thicker volume in your hands. Nevertheless, I will provide a bit of guidance.

Number One: A barfing cat with little or no prior history of vomiting may be really sick. Look for other symptoms, including things that may seem unrelated.

Your veterinarian may look like Dr. Dolittle. I'm sure he or she really does talk to the animals. I certainly do. But, sadly, animals don't talk back. That's why veterinarians rely heavily on the close observations of pet owners.

Yes, I'm trying to convince you to pay close attention to the how's and why's of your cat's vomiting. Don't let your cat down. Watch like a hawk and tell us what you saw. Take notes. When it comes to information, more is better.

One more thing: Don't waste a lot of time. Call the doctor's office and head on over. Don't wait for the folks at the front desk to say that the appointment schedule is full. Just go.

Number Two: A lot of cats vomit just now and then—you know, like it's a sport or something. I don't know about you, but I'd rather file my knuckles with a cheese grater than vomit. But cats aren't that averse to the whole process. For some of them, it's, like, "Well, the sun's out and the barometric pressure is 29.4 and rising so I guess I'll just heave right here." No apparent reason.

If it doesn't seem to happen often, you just wipe it up and life goes on. But here's the rub: Over time, it does occur with increasing frequency. And that creates a snowball effect. Each time your cat vomits, stomach acid is forced up into the esophagus. The stomach and small intestine become a little more inflamed. Then the cycle repeats, a little faster.

If you can still remember the last time that cat tossed his cookies, it's happening too often. I have a section on it in this very book. Even if all of the other cats do it, that doesn't make it OK. Invest in a thorough diagnostic workup and get it treated. Chronic vomiting never goes away by itself.

You'll find many more insights into this complicated phenomenon in Part 4 of this book.

RULE 8. Cats losing weight are quite sick.

Let's face it: A lot of us have fat cats. So, if they lose weight it's OK, right?

Well, the answer is, it's OK only if that kitty is losing weight because we want him to. Any cat (fat or thin) who starts to lose weight for no clear reason is in trouble. Unexplained weight loss is a problem that many cat owners try to forget or ignore.

In most cats, weight loss is a signal of chronic disease. The list of potential deadly causes is long and frightening. Common causes are kidney failure, malignant cancers, thyroid disease, intestinal disorders, feline AIDS, and leukemia. There are many more.

The moral of the story is that if you even *think* your cat is losing weight, immediately take her to the doctor. Even if you don't think it's serious enough to warrant an exam, ask the staff to weigh her for you. Chronic wasting diseases are often curable, or at least manageable.

If you kill time, you may kill your cat. When we are in denial, we may think we are effectively keeping our fears out of our minds, but our spirits are paying daily. Get your fears confirmed or erased—and trust your veterinarian to get the best possible result.

RULE 9. Cats don't "look out for themselves" more than dogs. They're just not very social creatures. They communicate less, but need every bit as much care. Always observe your cat closely.

By now I'm sure you realize that cats truly need careful monitoring by a knowledgeable owner to ensure that they don't get old before their time.

Sure, a great many cats have little or no medical history. There's a good reason in most cases: They're mixed breed. Just like human cultures—inbred individuals get weak. We see it in purebred dogs, horses, cattle, and royal families. But, fortunately, there has never been a major demand in our society for purebred cats. Nearly every cat in America is of such mixed parentage that they have "hybrid vigor."

That said, I should add that I've been a busy cat doctor for a long time, and I can tell you that with the way cats tend to hide illness and injury, they *need* us to care. I truly believe that most cats who have been assumed to have simply "run off to live with another family" actually hid out and died.

We need our cats. They need us, too. If you assume that their secretive nature is really a greater state of health, I'll bet you still believe that cats are really just dogs with short ears.

Wrong answer. Cats are cats.

RULE 10. Never strike a cat or speak harshly. Cats think we belong on a different planet anyway. To be a cat's friend, you must speak softly and carry a big menu.

Did I mention that cats are different than humans and dogs? Good. They are not socialized the way we are.

If you bawl out your cat very often, he will simply be an independent spirit someplace else.

I'm sure we've all noticed that the female pronoun is more commonly used when speaking of cats. We just assume that the cats are the girls and the dogs are the boys. Again, we are anthropomorphizing. We assign these different species human traits and then expect it to work. It goes along with the idea that the world was created in our image and likeness.

Sorry, not so. We humans are just one of millions of species meant to share this place. I don't mean to imply that we should never treat our pets like people. I think that's where the fun is. My pets have human names (well almost): Raoul is our cat and Peter Rabbit is our dog. They are like two more children in a family that shares everything. But I have taught my human children that they will never get a cat to relax and enjoy a relationship if they rush after him and grab him like a stuffed animal. Instead, they must sit quietly, speak softly, and wait.

RULE 11. Don't let your cat train you into feeding junk food. He already believes in his superior intelligence. Don't encourage him.

Remember the different sides of the same feline coin? Our indoor housecats are living out one aspect of their instinctive selves while the outdoor, free-living cats are simply displaying another essential facet of catdom. Whichever part your cat is playing, he or she needs to eat fairly frequently.

But wait, there's a paradox here. Clearly, the game-hunting, outdoor cat is much more active and thus burns many more calories than the house dweller. So why do indoor cats want to eat so much more?

The couch-potato cat isn't spending his time and mental energy sleuthing out his next snack. In fact, most indoor cats are just plain bored. If you're like many Americans today, boredom can be cured by food. A little bite for me, a little bite for my kittty—you know how it goes. The more you cater to your cat's tastes, the more fussy they become.

So, OK, we accept all that. But is it really important? So what if your cat is pleasingly plump?

Here's the problem: As cats gain weight, many will infiltrate their livers with fat. All seems to go well until they have reason not to eat—any minor stress can do it. But the body needs calories, so it breaks down the fat in liver storage and that cat starts a dangerous slide into potentially fatal liver failure. It's completely unnecessary.

So, save yourself and your kitty the heartache and be structured in some healthy, twice-daily measured feeding. Cure boredom with games and toys. (Elsewhere in this book, you'll find some tips for taking the boredom out of the life of a fat cat.) Just don't allow your cat to gradually convince you that she will wither away quickly without that canned salmon. That salmon is for you, the human, not for your feline friend.

PART 4

All Your Cat

Questions

Answered

Cat Age Compared to Humans

The old seven- years-to-one doesn't work—but this chart will help.

QUESTION:

Could you please tell me how to figure a cat's age? I know it isn't like everyone says, just 7 years for every 1 of ours.

DR. NICHOL:

Do our pets hang around the water bowl and debate their human's ages in pet years? I don't think so. But, heck, it's fun, so here's the chart:

CAT	HUMAN
1 year	15 years
2 years	24 years
5 years	36 years
7 years	45 years
12 years	64 years
15 years	76 years
18 years	88 years
21 years	100 years

For cats, this chart is a pretty good predictor of life expectancy. Still, many cats in their "seventies" can outrun a person of similar age. I say we should all stop counting. Life is short. Let's eat dessert first.

The Expense of Raising Cats

There are places to trim costs and do just fine. But if you cut quality on the wrong priorities, your pets will pay more later.

QUESTION:

Should I give vitamins to my pets? I have a whole menagerie. I have two guinea pigs, three cats, two dogs, and some fish. I try to feed good food but it can get expensive. So is it good to feed food that's just OK and add vitamins? Which vitamins are good?

DR. NICHOL:

I think I understand where you're coming from. A lot of us animal lovers surround ourselves with a whole family of pets. It's great to never be alone—and your pets are never alone either. I feel the same way. The down side, of course, is that good care for that many animals can get costly. What's important is to know where you can economize and where it's actually cheaper in the long term to spend the extra cash.

First, let's look at places to shave expenses. Cat litter is one. Since providing unused fresh litter is good prevention for urinary disease in cats, there is no point in a gold-plated latrine. Get the cheapest litter you can find, use very small amounts, and throw it away after every use. Canned pet food is another needless cost. Seventy-five percent of it is water and you pay about 20 cents just for the can. As for grooming, you can lose the shampoo in almost all cases and brush your pets instead. They like it, it's a great way to bond with them, and it's much healthier for their skin than bathing anyway. In fact a lot of folks clip their own dog's hair to save expense, too—although they might look like Gomer Pyle if you do. As for the guinea pigs, they don't really need cedar shavings for bedding. It's real nice but you can shred newspapers and they'll do fine as long as you replace it daily.

Now, here is where your pet-care dollars are best spent. Good food. I've said this before: When it comes to pet food, you will not get what you don't pay for. Compare ingredients and analysis if you must, but better diets have better digestibility. This means that your critters will absorb the nutrients they need much better and stay much healthier on better food. Will these diets work even better if you add vitamins? Not really. The real beauty of high-quality food (yes, good food is beautiful) is that it already has every important vitamin and mineral in the proper amount. If you add to a truly complete, balanced diet, you will throw it out of balance and actually diminish the nutritional plane of that pet.

So, what if you feed a mediocre diet? Will adding vitamins help? Sure. But you better also add everything else this diet lacks or you still won't make a real difference. Use good food in the first place and have peace of mind.

Now the exceptions: Guinea pigs must have vitamin C every day. Use the liquid supplement and add it to the drinking water. Follow the label instructions. Pets recovering from surgery or illness, or pets who are stressed due to a move to a new home, travel, or boarding are also good candidates for good-quality supplemental vitamins. Finally, working dogs, especially those who don't work hard consistently but only now and then. This includes hunting dogs, field trial dogs, and dogs who play professional sports like hockey and basketball. Treat these guys like stars. Feed the best food and give a good chewable multivitamin every day. Ask your veterinarian for a recommended brand.

Belly Buttons

Everybody has one. Here's how to find your cat's.

QUESTION:

Why don't cats have belly buttons like people?

DR. NICHOL:

Well, the truth is that they do, but they're just a bit more modest about them. I've examined the tummies of countless dogs, cats, ferrets, rabbits, hamsters, gerbils, rats, mice, and guinea pigs—and everybody has one but they are all strangely unfestooned with rings and studs and starburst tattoos. Each of them is discreetly covered with hair. Nonhuman mammals never seem to display their navels. I just don't get it.

To find your cat's belly button (navel/umbilicus), roll that baby on his or her back under a good light. It's located about one-third the distance between the rib cage and the pelvis. Cats are evenly haired, making locating this little vestige an even greater challenge. While none of us need a belly button after we leave the womb, that little scar serves as a reminder of the essential connection we had with our mothers that was the pipeline nourishment during our first months. I still love my mom.

Silent Dog Whistles and Your Cat

Cats can hear them, but—like most things canine—they lack dignity.

QUESTION:

I would like to know if a silent dog whistle is blown around my cat, will it bother her?

DR. NICHOL:

It is likely that your cat will ignore the "silent" dog whistle. The fact is that they aren't silent to dogs, nor to cats for that matter. The reason they hear the whistle and we inferior humans cannot is that these two species can detect higher pitched sounds than we can. What's nice about this type of whistle is that if you train your dog to come to you when you blow it, you can retrieve him without yelling or making other noise that might disturb other people. This means that when you use it, other dogs and cats will hear the sound as well. But like most noise we all hear everyday, the majority of it is meaningless unless one is conditioned to respond. Thus, your cat will view this high-pitched whistle as another of life's little mysteries to be pondered while waiting for the next lame mouse to hobble by. If your cat is the fussy type, she will make an annoyed cat face and tolerate more human absurdity like so much else. But don't expect her to come running and panting after you like a dog. She has far too much dignity for that. Why should she anyway—you're only human.

Where to Find Good Care for Your Cat When You're Out of Town

Leave out food and water? Friends who visit your home? Expensive kennels? Here's how to choose.

QUESTION:

Soon our children will be back in school and our family has one last vacation planned. We have a cat and a dog, but we don't know where to turn for reliable pet care while we're gone. Please advise us.

DR. NICHOL:

You show real concern for those other family members—your pets. Here are some bad ideas first. Do not leave a pet home alone (indoors or outdoors). It's Murphy's Law: Anything that can go wrong will. The water bowl gets dumped over, the critter gets stranded in the sun, or he or she gets sick and no one is there to care for him or her. Also, do not ask a neighbor child to stop over and feed and water. True, pets are great for teaching responsibility, but the wisdom to know when a pet is less than healthy is best left to an adult.

How about a few good ideas? A trusted adult friend to visit two or three times daily is usually fine. Another good option is a home pet-sitting service. Good pet-sitters are bonded and can provide references. Finally, there are boarding kennels for dogs as well as cats. Like most things in life, some are better than others.

How do you know who's good? Call your veterinarian's office and ask the staff for recommendations on pet-sitters and kennels. They've had experience with the good and the bad.

Be sure that whoever looks after your beloved pets has the phone number and name of your veterinarian and a number where you can be reached, too. If a problem does develop, we'll want your consent to take care of it right away.

Cats with Bells On

The noise doesn't cause hearing loss.

QUESTION:

I recently read in a cat magazine that you should not put bells on your cat's collar. The ringing, although an alarm for the birds and a locator for the owners, is very irritating and disorienting to a cat's sensitive hearing. Should I remove the bells from my cats' collars?

DR. NICHOL:

While cats haven't figured out how to remove the bells from their collars, it's clear that at least one of them has learned how to write for a cat magazine. Nice try, Fluffy, aka cat columnist. Brother!

I haven't found any information in the veterinary medical literature to suggest any health issues associated with cat bells. My experience in general practice (and as a feline audiologist) confirms this. Cats seem to adapt well to wearing a bell.

Why doesn't the noise drive them crazy? Remember that cats are not dogs with short ears. They are different. They are not constantly on the move. Cats by nature sit and wait most of their lives. In waiting, there is silence.

Microchips and Tattoos for Pet Identification

Each has its place, but microchips are the latest and greatest. They are quick to implant and highly reliable. Worth the modest expense.

QUESTION:

Are doctors trained to look for identifying tattoos and microchips? A friend of mine recently lost her Labrador Retriever—a very valuable show dog as well as a beloved pet—when he broke through the gate and took a walk. She hired the services of a search-and-rescue dog, advertised in the local newspapers, put up flyers all over the area, visited the humane society every day, and faxed information about the dog and his identifying tattoo to every veterinary clinic in the area. When she located this Lab after three and a half weeks, she was told that the dog had been neutered just a few days previous. The vet who did the neutering was told that the dog was a "stray." I hope that vets understand that a pet is a very important family member and that they should assist in attempting to reunite a lost animal with its family, much the same as we would work to reunite a lost child with his or her parents.

DR. NICHOL:

Wow. What a harrowing story. Your friend must have been not only worried sick, but also frustrated. Unless her Lab shows in obedience or tracking, being neutered takes him out of the game completely. You are right about the feelings we have for our pets. They are just like our children. Most of us work very hard to get the family back together when this kind of thing happens.

I will provide a bit of education for those who are not knowledgeable about microchips and tattoos. Both methods of identification are permanent and each has its advantages. A microchip is implanted by a quick injection of an inert glass-encapsulated, encoded device about the size of a grain of rice. It has no power source but will relay its unique code back to a "scanner" on a digital display. High tech. Microchips have been around for several years now and they have enormous value if the person who finds a pet gets him or her scanned. Since there is no way to know if a pet has a microchip under the skin, animal shelters are usually given free scanners by the manufacturers so they can scan every pet upon arrival. Pretty slick.

What about tattoos? You don't need fancy electronic gadgets to find them. (Ask anyone born after 1970.) But if you find one, who do you call? Unless your friend's dog had his owner's phone number on his inner thigh, the veterinarian may not have known where to go next.

What's better? I say both are better. If your local animal control facility (and veterinary hospital) has each of the different scanners and uses them all on every pet, and looks for tattoos, more lost pets will get home. But to make these systems work, we need a greater awareness. Here is what can be done: Call the National Dog Registry at 1-800-637-3647. Tell them you want information brochures that you can distribute to all area veterinary hospitals, shelters, boarding kennels, and grooming shops. Next, have your pets tattooed and/or implanted with microchips. Lastly, register their permanent identification with the National Dog Registry (they do cats, too). Then, if your lost pet's chip or tattoo gets called into these folks, they will provide your name and phone number to the caller. If you're real lucky, your dog or cat will arrive home still in possession of the family jewels.

A Single Cat in a Household
If he or she is a happy kitty, leave well enough alone.

QUESTION:

Our 7-month-old kitten spends approximately 12 hours a day alone. I worry that she gets lonely. I have been thinking about adopting another cat to keep her company. The kitten does get (demands, actually) plenty of attention from the dogs and people when we are all home. One of the dogs has a wonderful time sparring with the cat and chasing her up and down the stairs. So, do cats like feline company or are at least as happy on their own?

DR. NICHOL:

Cats by instinct are loners. That knowledge is based on a huge volume of observation by the behavioral and medical sciences. In addition, cats have been domesticated longer than any other pet. So, we feel strongly connected to our cats. But that sense of kinship and unconditional love causes us to make other assumptions that aren't always true. One false assumption is that cats enjoy a continuous party. Oh, sure, a cat will shake his booty once in a while. But the truth is that cats actually live a more monastic existence, often pondering the meaning behind all life.

Here are the harsh realities of life with more than one cat: If a cat feels crowded (many do with as few as one other cat in a home), they are more prone to urinating in places other than the litter pan. They are also at risk of physical illnesses like urinary and upper respiratory disease. And if they really hate each other, they are likely to always want to mangle the other—meaning that they will spit and howl at the most intriguing times of the day or night. Oh, how interesting the next 15 years will be for you and your husband if that happens.

You folks have one well-adjusted cat right now. You, your husband, and your dogs give this active youngster lots of attention and play. To give her even more stimulation, you can get a cat-climbing tree with carpet-covered houses and platforms. You can add a feathers-on-a-stick toy. She can race up and down, rip at it with her claws, and bat the feathers on a stick around. You're doing fine. Don't mess with a good thing and flirt with disaster.

Social Interactions

Even though cats are truly solitary creatures, they can still have social bonds. A great story of loving cats.

QUESTION:

A couple of weeks ago you wrote in your column that cats are political, not loving. It sounds like the people where I work, but it doesn't describe the cats I live with. I have two cats, Felix and Arthur, who treat each other with tenderness and concern.

Arthur tends to Felix when he is sick. Arthur will cuddle Felix for hours, with his paws around him. I've seen Felix approach Arthur to get his head licked. Of course, sometimes these lickings turn into chewings, but no harm is done. So, if you saw my cats curled up cheek to cheek in a heart shape on the bed, you would see that cats do have the ability to love.

DR. NICHOL:

This is an excellent perspective on feline behavior. Your life with Felix and Arthur clearly shows the complexity of the social interactions among housecats.

Cats are capable of many behaviors, sometimes serving as a model of caring, but in other cases causing injuries to each other or damage to their homes. In explaining the reasons for the problems, I often make generalizations. Cats are truly solitary and territorial by nature because they hunt that way in outdoor settings. But that does not mean they can't have social structures like a dominance hierarchy. As usual, it's easy for us to see their lives as an analogue of our own, as though they were an outgrowth of their owners. But that way of thinking leads to misconceptions. Cats are very unlike humans in many ways because they are a different species.

Your cats have an established relationship. The deference Felix shows Arthur means that Arthur is the likely dominant cat—which is OK. Human interaction that involves dominance smacks of office politics. But for our cats this structure forms the basis of the way they behave. Fortunately for everyone in your home, the social order of your cats, as well as that of the humans in the group, allows for the caring and nurturing that you get to share.

You have a truly beautiful family. We can't control the personalities of others, but we can foster love and bring out the best. Now, try that at work.

BITING AND FIGHTING

Biting During Play

How could a well-loved cat bite you while having a nice time?
How to correct it.

QUESTION:

Two years ago I acquired a Calico cat named Tiny. She is now 13 years old. (I love her.) She's sweet but when most affectionate, she bites. She also goes against the wall and seems to be crying—her tail goes almost straight up and it wriggles. Is she telling me something that I'm not getting?

DR. NICHOL:

We love our pets like children, but we forget that they are a different species. What Tiny is telling you is that she is a cat and you are not. Most humans neither attack and bite during play nor pretend to urinate against the wall. Tiny has a complex personality. She doesn't understand English, but she does communicate. Lucky for you, Tiny is not repainting your home with cat urine, but only going through the motions of normal territorial marking behavior.

Now for that naughty biting: Most cats who were weaned too early, then hand-raised by humans, were never taught self-control by their mothers. If Tiny nursed too hard, she would have been quickly reprimanded. Worse still, some cats stalk their owners and bite and claw as though they were hunting. Because the predatory stage in kitten development occurs right after they learn social play, a human-raised kitten never gets the lessons that only a mother cat can teach. Bummer. You live with a wild child that is lacking in social graces.

Rather than correcting the biting, we'll prevent it. Watch carefully as you play with Tiny. As soon as her ears begin to lay back, her claws extend, her tail switches, or her pupils dilate, startle her—but don't overdo it. I find that a strong cat-like hiss works well. As soon as she backs up a step, reward her quickly with a kitty treat or play gently with a feathers-on-a-stick toy to divert her attention from the aggressive attitude that you just derailed. Every time you play together, be ready to repeat this sequence—hundreds of times. Here is what *NOT* to do: *DO NOT* swat her on the nose. Her response will be an escalation of aggression that will damage your loving relationship. Tiny is a cat and not a person. She will only understand a cat-like correction. If you're firm and quick—and you don't get carried away— Tiny will eventually catch on.

Harassment Between Cats

A cat returning home from surgery can spark serious hostility.

QUESTION:

We found a stray kitten in our yard in early September. We couldn't find her owner so we kept her. Our 9-year-old neutered male cat Frodo has not been happy about this. Iggy, the kitten, is rambunctious and constantly harasses Frodo. Poor Frodo is constantly on guard, wondering when she'll get him next. Sometimes she is downright mean to him, and she frequently chases him from his favorite spots. This week, Iggy was gone for a day and a half to be spayed. Frodo was absolutely elated. He purred and played (which he hasn't done for a long time). When she returned, he growled and hissed even more than when we first found her. He's really upset.

We don't know what to do. We'd like to keep Iggy, but not at the expense of Frodo's sanity. We'd appreciate any suggestions you could give us.

DR. NICHOL:

Bummer, man. These two are acting, well, like a couple of cats. Now that I've stated the obvious, I'll try to help.

While we already know what Frodo would suggest, we can go back to the beginning and reintroduce these two—very slowly. To break the behavior pattern they have already established, Frodo and Iggy must be totally separated for two weeks. Then start the reintroduction by having one person hold each cat at opposite ends of a large room. While the cats are held, they will need a positive and enjoyable distraction like a game of "feathers on a stick." (Feathers on a stick is a cat toy sold in pet stores and some veterinary hospitals.) The idea is for each cat and handler to play individually. Do this for about ten minutes a couple of times a day. When it's clear that both cats are comfortable, move the games a few feet closer together. Play this way for several days or until both cats are relaxed, then move the play a little closer. Ultimately, if all goes well, they'll be playing side by side. When this close, but individual, playing has worked successfully for several days, try having them share one feathers-on-a-stick toy. If they are still doing well, you're still not done. (Sorry.) Your last big step will be to play with both using one toy for a few minutes, then remove the toy and watch. If they mix it up together, separate them and go back to the shared toy, or even separate toys, if necessary, to get them to relax again. But remember that, except for the training sessions, Frodo and Iggy must remain isolated from each other until it's clear that they will get along.

When they finally play nice together, you may be done. But if Iggy goes back to harassing poor Frodo, you may have to consider having their union annulled or maybe having Frodo take an assertiveness training class. But be optimistic. Many cats will buy into this behavior-modification plan. Admittedly some don't. If it fails, you know you have done your best. Yes, you can find a good home for Iggy.

Aggression Toward Other Cats and Skin Crawling

Complex problems may have multiple causes. Careful diet changes and management of medications are essential.

QUESTION:

I care for homeless cats (that's how I got five of my own—I love animals in general). One of my cats is Shanti who I got five years ago. He was so aggressive toward my other cats that he's been taking Megace for the last three years. It has helped immensely. He has another problem and that is of twitching along the spine. When this happens he licks his sides frantically. He runs through the house still licking as though something was stinging or biting him. He calms down in less than five minutes. One vet said he has hyperesthesia and put him on vitamin B complex. I tried this for a year and the problem remains, though it seemed to help. Any help you can give would be greatly appreciated.

DR. NICHOL:

You are definitely an animal lover to care for all those cats. I'm glad you found a way of managing Shanti's aggression. Now the poor guy has a different behavior problem. Let's see what we can do to help him.

Going back to Shanti's aggression with your other cats, it's no surprise that he improved on Megace. Megace is a synthetic form of the female hormone estrogen. It's quite reliable for this problem in male cats because of the direct connection between hormones and behavior in that species. (The truth is that all of us are influenced by our hormones, but we won't get that personal here.) While the Megace will continue to help Shanti be the sweet guy we all know him to be beneath his gruff exterior, there is a long-term risk. Cats given Megace for more than a few months may get malignant breast cancer—even a male. What's worse is that breast cancer in cats is nearly always a very nasty malignancy. But there are alternatives, so keep reading.

Poor Shanti also sounds like he really does have feline hyperesthesia syndrome. But before treatment is started, we need to be sure that it's not a result of excessive thyroid hormone levels instead. This problem, called hyperthyroidism, results from benign tumors of the thyroid glands and can also cause hyperactivity as well as a potentially fatal heart problem. So the first thing for Shanti to get is a thyroid test. If it's normal, we'll treat him for hyperesthesia.

There has been a bit of controversy about hyperesthesia in cats. Among the causes that have been considered are food allergy, epilepsy, and inflammation of nerves. There may be other causes, too, and more than one of them may be responsible in a particular kitty like Shanti. Because it's difficult to pinpoint the cause, different treatments may need to be attempted until the right one works in your cat.

Let's start with diet. Since food allergies are usually due to the protein source, prescription hypoallergenic diets for cats have meats like venison or duck. (Sounds pretty good, doesn't it?) The brand name that is most recommended by veterinary dermatologists is IVD—your veterinarian can get it for you. To do what's called a therapeutic trial, give Shanti the IVD diet for eight weeks allowing him nothing else but water. To accomplish this, you'll need to feed all of your cats separately. If he's better, you have a diagnosis. What if it doesn't work? We can do another therapeutic trial but with a drug called phenobarbital which is often used for treatment of epilepsy. If that fails, we can try diazepam, Buspar, or even prednisone. One way or another, we are very likely to manage Shanti's hyperesthesia.

While you can be confident that we can help your kitty stop chasing himself around your house, the best possible result would be to find that the same treatment would also manage his aggression. If you continue with the Megace, you could end up losing him to breast cancer. Instead, ask his doctor to start him on diazepam for his aggression and stop the Megace. Then try the diet or another medication. When both problems are under control, try quitting the diazepam. When it comes to drug therapy, less is more.

Aggressive Mother Cat

Behavior toward the kittens can change after weaning and spaying. Improvement must come with skill and patience.

QUESTION:

Last summer our 1-year-old female cat had a litter of kittens. We wanted her to have the kittens, we had already found homes for them, except for the two we wanted to keep. She was a very good mama and we had to force her to stop nursing the two we kept. A couple of months after the babies were born, we had mama spayed. At first she was fine, then she started growling and spitting at the babies and us, too, which almost a year later she still does. Also she will bite. Sometimes she acts fine and other times she's acting like she has PMS. I had her checked over by our vet and he can't find anything physically wrong with her. She's quite the Bitch—what can we do??

DR. NICHOL:

Mama cat has two separate problems. For one thing, she is responding to the increased number of cats in your home. Since cats are loners by nature, she is feeling stressed by having so many other adult cats in her territory. While this may seem illogical since the additional cats are her babies, remember that after she raised them, she assumed they would be leaving home to attend college, find jobs, or at least get married. (No wonder she's grumpy.) Second, she also has what's called redirected aggression, that is, aggression toward people. This latter problem is related to the first in that she is simply feeling overwhelmed. Now that I've confused you with what's wrong with Mama, I will help you fix it.

For starters, avoid all activities that might trigger Mama's aggression. If it might get her honked off, don't do it. Next, separate her from the other cats. To help her calm down and to speed the process, it would help to temporarily give Mama an anti-anxiety drug like amitriptyline or diazepam. Following this we'll do counterconditioning and desensitization, which in English means we will allow Mama and the other cats to see each other only from long distances at first. While they are glowering at one another, we will feed them little tidbits to show them that the pleasure they feel as they eat may really be associated with their former enemy. As they become a bit more civilized in their regard for each other, we will shorten the distance between them as we continue with the delectable morsels.

But what about you—the one who's making all of this possible? You get to play a game called feathers-on-a-stick—but not yet. First, do nothing until Mama comes to you. Then rebuild your friendship with her by tossing little bits of food to her. When she starts to feel like you might be an OK human after all, glue some feathers to the end of a stick (you can actually buy a toy like this) and gently play with her until she really warms up. As you play, gradually reduce the distance between you and her until she rediscovers the deep wonder of your magnetic personality.

Will this work? I can say with confidence that it will. I have employed these methods in other cases and they are sound. So get out there and whip those cats into shape—and enjoy the feathers.

Breeding and Reproductive Organs

■ ■

Reproduction in Cats and Kittens

When the hormones hit and what to do about it.

QUESTION:

At what age can a kitten become pregnant? My kitten is 4 months old. I am baby-sitting a male kitten who looks about 8 months old.

DR. NICHOL:

Gee, the girl is 4 months old and the young stud is 8 months: sounds more like puppy love to me. Should you be worried? Is this "age appropriate"? Is it even legal? What if a pregnancy resulted from this tawdry little affair? Would it be "Kittens having kittens"?

OK, let's not take this too seriously. Here is the rest of the story: Most male and female cats reach sexual maturity at about 6 months of age. Because of the reduced number of daylight hours this time of year [autumn/winter], your young flower may not come into "heat" until early spring. In addition, cats—as well as rabbits—are "spontaneous ovulators," meaning that they do not release an ovum (egg) on a set schedule like most other mammals. For example, we humans have a female reproductive cycle of 28 days, dogs about 6 months, etc. But cats, on the other hand, won't ovulate until they are bred by a lothario such as that visitor of yours. This means that nearly every breeding with cats results in more kittens.

Do you need to be worried about this? At 4 months, your little girl still thinks boys are yucky. But if these two are still an item in a couple of months I would recommend one or more of the following: (1) spay your kitten, (2) neuter the male, or (3) send your girl to live at a convent.

Different Fathers for the Same Litter

Because each sperm (even from different fathers) fertilizes a separate egg, there can be a different father for each kitten in a litter. But that mother cat can have other litters of kittens all fathered by the same male.

QUESTION:

Our purebred Siamese cat came into heat last week and we bred her to a male Siamese. But as soon as she came home from being bred, she got out of the house and we found her hanging out with this nasty-looking alley cat. Her name is Rosie and I know that her purebred kittens would be beauties, but what if she got bred by this alley cat? Will he ruin the whole litter? Could having mixed-bred kittens once ruin her for purebred litters next time?

DR. NICHOL:

Your cat Rosie is typical of cats in heat (that time of the female's reproductive cycle when ovulation occurs). The hormone levels in her body not only cause the release of several ovum (eggs), but hormones are also responsible for causing her to attract male cats as well as to go out in search of them. If Rosie were bred by both tomcats, you may have some kittens in the litter with different fathers. Here's why.

Since it requires one ovum (egg) and one sperm to make an embryo (the earliest stage of development), there will be as many embryos as there are eggs that get fertilized by sperm. If Rosie releases six ovum and they all get fertilized, there will be six kittens. But the ovum are not released all at the same time. So if she releases the six eggs over a few days, and she is bred first by the Siamese tomcat and later by the alley cat, you are likely to get some kittens who are purebred and some who are half Siamese and the other half mixed bred. Of course, they all have genes from Rosie because she is the mother of all of them. But some will have genes from one father while others will have genes from the other father.

What about future litters? There is never any lasting affect from the genetic input from a previous father. So you can breed her to any male you want after this. But you are not the first cat owner to notice how *badly* an in-heat cat wants to get bred. Even cats who have been frightened of the outside will throw caution to the wind when in heat.

By the way, you shouldn't have trouble placing the mixed-bred kittens in good homes. A "Free to good home" ad in the classified section of the newspaper should get the job done. But I would advise that you leave out the part about their mother being a floozy.

Spaying an Indoor Cat

What's the point if they never go outside? Surging hormones cause major behavior changes in cats. When nature calls, your kitty will find a way to reproduce.

QUESTION:

My cat Misty really means everything to me. She stays inside all the time. There is no way for her to get pregnant, but I am told that it is still a good idea to get her spayed. How could it be so important? She is like a child to me. I am really afraid that she might not come through the surgery.

DR. NICHOL:

I understand how you feel about Misty. You are not alone. It turns out that 70 percent of pet owners consider their pets as children. Most veterinarians feel just as strongly. First, I will tell you why spaying is important, then I will tell you about the risk.

As much as Misty is strictly indoors, she may have a major attitude change when she comes into her first "heat" period. The hormone changes make many of these girls suddenly want to go out and find a tomcat as fast as possible. No kidding. Even if she simply cannot get out, remaining unspayed puts her at risk of breast cancer later. This tumor is malignant 90 percent of the time in cats—and it's remarkably aggressive and fast growing. The bottom line is that spaying makes sense.

How about the risk? This is a real important question. First, there is never a guarantee. But her chances of a healthy recovery are very close to 100 percent if she has the following. First, a preanesthetic lab profile to be sure that her internal organs are working fine. Second, high safety gas anesthesia given with oxygen. Third, be sure to ask the doctor if there will be an IV catheter in place (just in case), and lastly a heart monitor for the staff to know that Misty is doing well throughout the procedure.

The real question is: Do the benefits outweigh the risks? If done properly, the answer is a definite yes.

Pregnancy in Cats

Do the right things early to ensure a healthy mama and babies.

QUESTION:

My $1\frac{1}{2}$-year-old cat is pregnant (about two months). I just wanted to know how long pregnancy will be and is there any prenatal care that should be given. I also believe she has a tapeworm.

Dr. Nichol:

Pregnancy in cats lasts 63 days (about two months). Most signs like a swollen tummy and development of the mammary glands don't appear until the last two to three weeks. The best diet for your girl is a high-quality dry kitten food because it will provide the optimum calcium/phosphorus ratio as well as a bit of extra protein. The best is Health Blend by Hills available from your veterinarian. While you're there, have her thoroughly examined.

Tapeworms: Your cat has them either from fleas or from eating rodents. They cannot pass directly to the babies. Fleas can. The babies can be at risk from the fleas because they can be bled to death by these blood-sucking insects. If you see fleas, get a flea powder with carbaryl from your veterinarian's office for use on mama and the babies. Do not use tapeworm treatment before the babies are weaned. Tapeworms are worth treating, but are not really a significant risk. I would suggest having a stool sample checked for other parasites. Vaccinations should also wait until after the babies are born.

Now my questions for you: Who is the father of this family? Does he have a good job or does he just spend his time chasing mice around? Is he this "tapeworm"?

CANCERS

■ ■

Vaccination-Related Cancers

The risks and rewards of vaccination. Now we know that less may be better.

QUESTION:

Our 12-year-old cat has developed a pea-sized lump at the site of the vaccination she got last November. We have since found out about post-injection fibrosarcoma and are afraid she now has cancer. Should we have it biopsied? We've heard that a biopsy may cause it to spread more rapidly if it is cancer. We're concerned about the risk of having her under general anesthesia.

DR. NICHOL:

Oh, brother. This is a tough one. For the past 40 years veterinary medicine has heavily lobbied the American public to protect their pets against every disease possible. Recently, more vaccines have been added to the "distemper combination." These have been repeated year after year in cats like yours. It sounds good, but there is more to the story.

While modern medicine is great, there are risks. Annual repetition of the same vaccines can make rare sarcomas (cancers) more likely in some cats—and these malignancies can be aggressive. Proceed quickly. Ask your veterinarian to do a geriatric health screen first. If it's normal, move ahead with anesthesia and have that mass removed and evaluated to make sure it's been totally eliminated. Want to avoid anesthesia? A needle aspirate of the tumor can give us useful information—but you're right, it could cause a malignancy to get "fired up" and spread faster. But if you act quickly with surgery, you can cure your kitty of a potential killer.

Recently it's becoming clear that with vaccinations, more is not necessarily better. For many adult cats it might be wise to vaccinate against a different infectious disease each year rather than every disease every year. Your veterinarian can recommend the safest protection.

Don't take this to mean that cats are better off without vaccinations—the risk is small. An annual exam may be the best way to make sure your pets do well long term. We'll keep doing our best. I'll keep you posted.

Leukemia Virus

What are the risk factors? How to avoid trouble.

QUESTION:

I have two cats who I've had vaccinated against leukemia who come into contact with other cats. There are two neighbor cats who had been diagnosed positive for feline leukemia and neither cat has been put to sleep. How dangerous is it for my cats?

DR. NICHOL:

Ready for a complicated answer? Feline leukemia virus (Felv) is a contagious cancer-causing organism. It can also lead to several other diseases that are potentially fatal. But it's not highly infectious except in some circumstances.

An infected cat carries Felv in the blood, saliva, stool, and semen. During active infection, it can spread to another cat through a transfusion; breeding; mutual grooming activities; shared food, water, and litter pans; and—most important for your cats—fight wounds. Some cats die from it and some get over it on their own. Others can be lifelong carriers or latent cats where the virus moves back and forth from the blood to the bone marrow. Confused? Good.

Those neighbor cats are a threat to your cats only if the virus is active in their blood. But your two are vaccinated, right? That's good, but until recently leukemia vaccination has been only about 60 percent effective. A new vaccine just released claims 95-percent efficacy, but time will be the judge. Real protection for your cats depends on their relationships with these local pariahs. Do they physically feud or just call one another ugly names? Do they know them in the biblical sense? Will these other hoods submit to random blood testing? Would your cats be happy staying indoors? Avoidance of a known risk is the best protection.

Skin Lumps on Cats

Do not "wait and see." Most are malignant. Early surgery can save Fuzzball's life.

QUESTION:

I am writing you today to ask if you can help with any suggested treatment for a member of our family. His name is Fuzzball, a 13-year-old male cat who looks like "Sylvester" the cat. Some months ago, we noticed Fuzzball was walking with a slight limp favoring his right arm. The limp persisted and did cause him pain. A visit to our regular vet could find no problem. He was put on Tolfedine. This helped the pain. A few days later, I noticed a small-sized lump on his right elbow. X-rays were taken as well as a fine-needle aspirate. Diagnosis: Mixed inflammation with prominent eosinophilic component.

Fuzzball was given a Depo Medrol injection and put on Cephalexin. It was thought we would notice a change, but it has remained the same and his arm hurts. Our doctor cannot offer any further treatment other than "wait and see." We feel an operation is not an option as the lump looks like it is interfering with either a nerve, muscle, or tendon. Doctor, with your experience and the information given, can you offer any suggestions for treatment or know anyone to whom you can refer me? Thank you so much for your time. Fuzzball really means a lot to us.

DR. NICHOL:

I can tell this is very hard for you. After 13 years most of us would be just as attached to such a precious friend as Fuzzball. With that kind of emotional commitment, it is nearly impossible for you to be objective enough to make good treatment decisions. So, let me be the detached third party for you. Your cat Fuzzball has a serious problem. Not only is he in pain, but his leg is not functioning properly.

The medications that were tried were logical choices based on the pathologist's diagnosis from the needle aspirate. They were intended to manage infection and inflammation. Why didn't they work? First, understand what a fine-needle aspirate is and what it is not. The procedure is simple. The needle is inserted into the interior of the mass and a few cells are "aspirated" (sucked) into the inside of a syringe. The cells are put on a glass slide and sent to a pathologist who simply reports what is seen under the microscope. It sounds like an easy way to get a diagnosis. But remember that the needle aspirate is nothing more than a blind stab. What if the inside of the lump isn't consistent throughout? What if that tiny sample showed cells that didn't truly represent the whole tumor? Yes, it may be a tumor.

Poor Fuzzball is still in trouble, so we have to put this boy right. It's time to consider the worst-case scenario and make whatever decision is needed. Consider that 85 percent of all skin tumors in cats are malignant—usually aggressively so. Even if you act quickly, you may find that the mass is too advanced to be completely eliminated. But if the mass is surgically removed, the pathologist can examine the whole thing and provide an accurate diagnosis. If the report shows that there is more cancer still remaining on Fuzzball, there may still be options like amputation (cats do remarkably well—believe it) or chemotherapy (they handle that with few complaints). On the other hand, surgical removal alone could be curative.

I know how hard it is to digest this kind of advice. What about anesthetic safety on an older kitty? What if the tumor involves a nerve? For you to save your beautiful Fuzzball, you will need to be brave and accept some risk. Ask your veterinarian for a referral to a trained surgeon. Go for the gold. Save your cat.

Fuzzball's Saga Continues . . .

QUESTION:

Thank you for taking the time to reply to my questions about Fuzzball. Here is an update. Fuzzball went in for surgery to have the mass in his elbow removed. The mass had grown around a nerve and artery and was not possible for our vet to remove without the fear of him ever being able to walk on that limb again. A biopsy was taken. The diagnosis: adenocarcinoma, possibly metastatic.

Please, if you have any suggestions, or know of anyone who could help, let me know. We don't have anything to lose. Fuzzy came home from surgery the same day and immediately started chasing birds off our lawn. He eats well and shows no signs of discomfort, but I know he will get worse and that's unbearable for me to accept. I was told radiation or chemotherapy would not help and only cause him discomfort and stress. I just cannot sit back and do nothing. I have to try and find some way to help my friend. Thank you again for your time.

DR. NICHOL:

It's great to hear that Fuzzball is up and around and active. While it's excellent that he is feeling well, as you know, we are not done with his cancer yet. The information from the biopsy is invaluable. We now know what we must do to give Fuzzy his best shot at survival.

Adenocarcinomas by definition are malignancies that are derived from glandular tissue. The cancer Fuzzball has may have started with a sweat gland. Because the entire tumor was not removed, the pathologist can't tell us everything about it. While the elbow tumor may have already spread, this mass by itself could be a cancer-spread lesion. But that's worse-case scenario. Best case is that the malignancy is still confined to Fuzzy's elbow. X-rays of his chest and abdomen as well as aspirates of his lymph nodes may show cancer spread. But if they all show negative, I say go for broke: Amputate the leg.

Holy smoke! Isn't that drastic? There are two essential points here. The first is that this is the only way to save the life of your beautiful cat. If you back out now, you can count on losing him soon. Second, cats do just fine with three legs— honest. Fuzzball will be happily chasing birds on three legs.

Anything else? Once the entire mass is removed, the pathologist can examine every bit of it. The cancer will be methodically described and graded as to its degree of aggressiveness. Chemotherapy following surgery may be useful. This is not to be feared. While people often have a bad time, cats and dogs seldom have any complaints at all. The key to all of this is putting Fuzzball in the hands of a doctor who is knowledgeable in cancer surgery and treatment. If there is no such veterinary facility nearby, ask Fuzzy's doctor for a referral. Last, act quickly. Time is *not* on your side.

Fuzzball: The Final Frontier . . .

QUESTION:

I wanted to bring you up-to-date on Fuzzball's condition. He underwent surgery to remove the forelimb with the cancerous elbow. He has some adapting to do, but I know he will do fine. Thank you again for your encouragement, and I look forward to receiving any suggestions you have for after surgery and future care I can provide.

Dr. Nichol:

Thanks for the update. You and Fuzzball have shown great courage in committing to his longer life by having the amputation done. I know it was a hard decision. Fuzzball will adapt quickly all by himself. Cats are remarkable this way. Could this tumor show up elsewhere in his body? Yes, but it's unlikely. It's a reminder to us all to live life to the fullest every day. God bless you both.

Breast Cancer in Cats

An aggressive killer, breast tumors in cats must be removed ASAP. All lumps on kitties need immediate attention.

Question:

I have a cat and her name is Katy. Katy is 13 years old. She has always stayed inside, so we never got her spayed. A few weeks ago I found a lump under her belly and I thinks it's getting bigger. Does Katy need a vet?

Dr. Nichol:

It sounds like you and Katy are very close and that you have taken good care of her for a long time. With the problem she has now, you must act quickly.

The first thing Katy needs is a complete physical exam. My greatest concern is that she may have breast cancer. If the mass you describe is located on one of her breasts (mammary glands), it must be surgically removed immediately. The reason is that breast cancer in cats is malignant in about 95 percent of cases and it is remarkably aggressive. These are the basics, but there is a bit more to it.

While surgery is Katy's best hope, it's important to understand the possible advancement of the disease first. The place to begin is with three X-ray views of her chest. This is essential to check for spread of the cancer to her lungs. If we don't see any tumors, we may have a fighting chance. Next, a complete blood and urine screening is necessary to make sure her organ function is good. If this checks out as well, we go to surgery with the plan to take a wide area of tissue surrounding the cancerous gland. We also remove the other mammary glands, usually taking some of the normal ones two to three weeks later.

Will this save Katy for you? That's a tough question. If the pathology report shows that her cancer is an aggressive malignancy, chemotherapy should follow the surgery. While this approach will extend her life expectancy, she may still die from this ugly disease. On the other hand, if the pathologist feels that the entire disease was removed at the time of surgery, Katy may be home-free.

I know this sounds scary. Be brave and have your beloved Katy examined right away. It's her best hope. My last point is for other cats you may have. Don't assume that spaying is only for outside cats who are likely to get bred and have kittens. Spaying every cat when she is young is highly likely to prevent this angry cancer.

Second Opinions and Chemotherapy

Anxiety, fear, and doing the right thing for a beloved pet. Where to start and what's right for you and your kitty.

QUESTION:

My cat's 13 years old and she's been losing weight and eating poorly for a few weeks. My husband and I have no children and this little cat means the world to us. Yesterday we took her to her vet who did some tests. She said that "Spider" has cancer and that she needs chemotherapy. This is very upsetting. We want a second opinion. But who do we see? Are there specialists?

DR. NICHOL:

I am so sorry about Spider. You are not alone in your feelings. News like that is hard to take. Maybe the first veterinarian is wrong, maybe not. Those of us who consider our pets as children never want to hear the word cancer. I know how frightened you must feel.

I will try to give you some perspective. Number one: Please do not feel that you are betraying your veterinarian when you want confirmation of a diagnosis or treatment plan. On the other hand, try first to understand whether it is a need to be sure, or the possibility that you never trusted this doctor in the first place. Or consider that maybe you liked the doctor until you were given bad news. Either way, your feelings are legitimate.

Are there specialists? Yes. To know where to turn, consider asking the first veterinarian. If she is a true professional (and most of us are), she will understand that you are speaking from your heart when you ask for more help. Tell her that it is your love for your pet that motivates your need for consultation. Since Spider's doctor's first concern is for her patient's well being, she is duty bound to help you find a knowledgeable second opinion. In addition, she is obliged to provide copies of records for the second doctor.

Two final points: Try hard to put aside your anxiety over Spider's condition when talking to her doctor. Veterinarians have feelings, too. Be kind. Lastly, ask the doctor to send or fax the records directly to the other doctor rather than insisting on taking the copies yourself. This will preserve your relationship with the first doctor by showing her that you trust her. Good faith really counts.

Cat-Human Diseases

Allergies to Pets

Here are several hypoallergenic cat breeds.

QUESTION:

I would like to know if a child is allergic to cats, does it necessarily mean dogs, also?

DR. NICHOL:

I think you're great to find a pet for your children. Pets teach love and forgiveness in ways that no parent can. Peter Rabbit and Raoul (our family dog and cat) have a big place in the lives of the Nichol boys. But asthma and inhaled allergies in children can be dangerous.

Cats: Glad you asked. What good is life without a cat? The best breeds are Sphinx and Rex cats because they have less hair. Of the three varieties of Rex cats—Cornish, Devon, and Selkirk—the first two are better for cat allergies. While Sphinx cats are less hairy and nonflaky, they are quite oily and need frequent baths.

The species of pets are different. If your child has trouble with any or all cat and dog breeds, consider a reptile or a pocket pet like a gerbil. Or even a Chia pet. But for heaven's sake, get that kid a critter.

Hantavirus

A disease of pets and humans, the human risk is low—mostly.

QUESTION:

I live in the Four Corners area and camp in the mountains in the Flagstaff area. The hantavirus has been reported in Arizona and I am concerned about our pets. Can they catch the virus and/or transfer it to humans?

DR. NICHOL:

I'm glad you're concerned about hantavirus. This infection has actually been around for a long time. It infects about 150,000 humans each year in Europe and Asia—with 5 percent of those cases being fatal. The West was introduced to this sneaky virus during the Korean Conflict when our soldiers became affected in the Hantaan River valley.

Sounds pretty ugly—but there's more. Most of what has been learned about hantavirus relates to rodent populations and accidental human exposure to their urine and feces. What has happened to the Navajo people in your area largely seems to have resulted from exposure to accumulated dust mixed with the dried urine and droppings of deer mice in confined areas, like a seldom-used shed. Accidentally disturbing these rodent nesting areas releases the virus into the air. Thus, a person who inhales the virus can easily get pneumonia-like symptoms. But the fatal part of the equation is often from the spread of the virus to the kidneys. It's a real serious disease.

So what's the risk to you and your pets when camping? Not much. Yes, you may have a chance encounter with an infected deer mouse while you commune with nature—and cats, dogs, and humans can get hantavirus. But you will need to inhale a pretty strong concentration of the virus to get sick. To avoid this disease, just don't you or your pets go sticking your noses (literally) into accumulations of mouse urine and droppings. Dogs and cats will hunt rodents. If they raid a rodent nest, they might become infected. Ultimately that could put you at risk if you contact their urine or stool. The risk is small. Be safe and keep your pets under control and don't hassle those poor deer mice. Those poor dears had it rough with all the media attention they've already had over this thing.

Heartworms and Human Risk

We are not the normal host for this parasite. But carrier mosquitoes have infected a few unlucky folks.

QUESTION:

Can people get heartworms? If dogs and cats get it from mosquitoes, can't humans?

DR. NICHOL:

Cases of human infection with *Dirofilaria immitus* (heartworm) has occurred, but it is pretty rare. The reason is that the human immune system is very good at killing the larvae because we are not a natural "host" for this parasite—like dogs. Cats are less commonly infected than dogs, but it isn't rare in cats. It is for this reason that a once-a-month tablet has been developed and approved for use as a feline heartworm preventative. If you are concerned about the safety of your cat, ask your veterinarian for more information.

DESTRUCTIVE BEHAVIORS

Chewing

Chewing and sucking on fabric can be prevented by providing wholesome after-school alternatives.

QUESTION:

Our 9-month-old kitten has one bad habit. She chews holes in things like the comforter cover, my sweat pants, and socks when no one is around. Do you know why she would be doing this and can you recommend action we can take?

DR. NICHOL:

Is this "Stump the Expert"? Like many cat behaviors, destructive chewing may be manageable by any one of several changes you need to make. What will work on your kitty depends partly on how motivated she is to destroy your home.

For starters, keep the stuff she has already chewed away from her. Closing doors into bedrooms while you're gone would make good sense. Next, provide her plenty of wholesome activities like a cat-climbing tree. Attach a feathers-on-a-stick toy. In addition, hard dry food helps deflect domestic destruction by giving the cat something useful to chew. Lastly, you can provide her some catnip toys and a kitty herb garden. The plants in the herb garden are healthy if she consumes them and cats think they're fun to destroy. If all that fails, get her a computer game and let her play with the mouse.

Furniture Wrecking

Clawing upholstery is taboo. Declawing is one option—but there are some good alternatives.

QUESTION:

My cat Willie is turning into a real problem child. I have had this boy for over a year and we have gotten quite close. But more and more he is destroying my furniture. He seems to know everytime my back is turned. Then he sneaks off and claws the new sofa. I've tried a squirt gun and throwing keys at him, but he seems to thinks it's a game. Is declawing the answer? It sounds cruel.

DR. NICHOL:

You have raised an important question. I'm sure you have considered making Willie an outdoor cat. Many cats make this transition well, but I would not push you to make this decision: Outdoor cats have a shorter life expectancy. Instead, let me give you some options and you can choose.

In terms of negative reinforcement, you have another choice. It's called a Scat Mat. These are available through a couple of mail-order sources and come in a few different sizes. You put it on the sofa and plug it into a wall outlet. It will give Willie a low-voltage, static electricity-like shock when he touches it. It won't work on every cat, but it could eliminate the need to declaw Willie. It's much better to have a device like a Scat Mat punish Willie than for you to do it. As much as he thinks it's a game, you don't want to damage your relationship with your cat. Besides, a gizmo like this is faster than you are and will catch him every time.

What about surgery to declaw Willie? It is actually not a bad option. If you find that this little weasel outsmarts your Scat Mat (not likely, but possible), declawing could make the difference between keeping Willie or finding him another home. Is it painful? Young cats seem to have discomfort for only one to two days postoperatively. This will not be significant given the pain relievers that we use right after surgery. If you feel that Willie will need these at home, too, be sure to ask his doctor to dispense tablets. For this procedure we like to use Torbutrol tablets in our hospital. They are safe, reliable, and free of side effects.

Whatever you do, stay away from aspirin, ibuprofen, and especially acetaminophen (Tylenol). This stuff is truly deadly in cats.

Chewing Plastic and Other Nonfood Items

Indoor cats get bored and need healthy activities. Provide wholesome activities or say goodbye to your nice stuff.

QUESTION:

I have two young cats, ages 1 year and about 9 months, and a third, nearly geriatric. Of the young cats, the older one chewed a lot of plastic when he was around 6 months old (including a portable phone!), but he wasn't particular—he also chewed cardboard. Now the younger one has been caught chewing plastic (including the cord to my carbon monoxide detector!). My old cat isn't a problem. Is this because their permanent teeth are on the way? Will cats take a liking to those dorky plastic pork-chop dog toys or should I spray catnip on one of those rawhide things?

DR. NICHOL:

Your questions are important. Aside from the damage to your phone and other appliances, there are some definite risks to your cats if this continues.

Why do they like plastic? Number one: Since the adult teeth in kittens are already in place by age 6 months, I doubt this is a result of new teeth. But until kittens are over 1 year of age, they have a great deal of energy. Like little kids, they get into trouble unless you provide healthy after-school activities like sports or arts and crafts. Otherwise, they join gangs and chew plastic.

What's so bad about plastic? Aside from pieces of it getting lodged in the stomach or intestines, the act of biting the electric cord on your carbon monoxide detector is most worrisome. Cats who bite electric cords can get severe burns of the mouth that can cause their tongues to slough. So it's definitely a habit worth stopping if only to prevent a smoldering cat from generating more carbon monoxide.

To manage this deviant behavior, start with a good diet. Remember that you will know the good stuff by the price. Cheap food is poorly digestible, causing a cat to chew things other than cat food. Next, get some really fun toys like a cat tree. This is a carpet-covered, multileveled playhouse affair. I recommend one that is tall enough to reach the ceiling. All of your cats will enjoy scampering around and playing hide and seek. In addition, you can hang other toys like feathers-on-a-stick from the platforms. But while these things are good fun, there's still nothing like the taste of plastic.

So, what can you do if you provide the greatest alternatives, but they still go after plastic? Hide the plastic. If the object is immovable, put a Scat Mat in front of it. But break that habit. Don't wait for them to quit on their own.

Oh, about those dorky plastic pork-chop dog toys? Forget it. If you're a cat, *everything* dog-like is dorky.

Declawing

Concerns about post-surgical pain are important. We can help.

QUESTION:

Victoria Louise is a 7-year-old, pretty fat tabby who is an expert furniture shredder. She's just smart enough to know that she will be sprayed with water and shrieked at if she claws in our presence. I have heard that a cat will not walk the same, might have a personality change, and will certainly be in major pain for weeks if her claws are removed. This cat is precious to me, and I don't want to warp her for life. I hope I will not end up with a psycho.

Dr. Nichol:

Ah, the well-loved problem child. You needn't worry; she can have an excellent recovery. For adult cats a Duragesic skin patch, applied the day before surgery, will give three to four days of pain relief. Any follow-up pain can be easily managed using Torbugesic mixed with tasty VAL syrup and given orally. Lose the guilt trip. Our pets are in our lives to share our love, not to destroy our stuff. Besides, Victoria Louise will like you better if you stop trying to extinguish her like a forest fire.

[**Note:** I believe it's best to avoid declawing, and I've often advised cat owners on different methods of discouraging destructive behavior. But while many cats can be trained, a few are not amenable to any changes. In fact, there are cats who scratch members of their families, including children. Sometimes declawing is the only way to prevent a cat from being taken to a shelter. All things considered, it isn't a bad last resort.]

EARS

■ ■

Earflap Swelling

Head shaking/ear scratching can damage blood vessels in the earflaps, forming a blood pocket. Treatment of the disease of the ear canal is priority one.

QUESTION:

I have a 5-year-old cat. He had been holding his ear down, and when we looked at it, the entire inside is swollen. It looks like a bubble. I don't want to take him to the vet for something that will clear up on its own! It doesn't seem to bother him at all, not even when we touch it! It just looks awful! Please help!

DR. NICHOL:

You are describing an auricular hematoma. It is a non-painful pocket of blood that has filled the space between the cartilage and skin of the pinna (earflap). As much as it is abnormal, by itself it's not a major problem. The greater concern is its cause. This hematoma, or blood pocket, has formed because your kitty has ear pain and has been doing some serious head shaking and ear scratching. So much, in fact, that the tiny vessels inside the earflap have broken and leaked enough blood to cause a swelling. The reason for his pain is a problem way down inside the ear canal close to the eardrum. The usual causes are things like bacterial or yeast infections, ear mites, ticks, and foxtail awns. The bottom line is that you will need to make that dreaded trip to the veterinarian. If left untreated, the pain and infection will only worsen.

Now, back to the hematoma of the earflap. This part does not require treatment. If you get the ear canal managed, you can ignore the flap if you want to. It'll heal by itself if you do nothing about it, but it will be permanently rumpled like a leaf of iceberg lettuce. The alternative to this vegetation of the head is a minor surgical correction that will preserve your cat's boyish good looks. You make the call on the earflap.

Ear Infections

They can recur time and again. Get serious. End the misery for the kitty and protect long-term health.

QUESTION:

My father's cat has a problem since birth with his ears. He seems to have what we thought at first was some sort of ear mite and now believe to maybe being some sort of a yeast infection in his ears. He will constantly shake his head and stuff does come out and his ears are very sensitive. My father has tried various products and it seems once it gets cleared up, the problem comes right back.

DR. NICHOL:

Well, I'm glad to get this question. I can tell you from a lot of experience (25 years) what a major problem ear infections can be. It's the most common disease we treat. But when they get deeply rooted and advanced, they can be difficult to cure because of permanent changes in the anatomy of the ear canal caused by chronic inflammation.

Your dad's cat sounds like he's been miserable for a long time. And his infections may be due to more than one cause. Foreign material like ticks, mites, and foxtail awns could have been the inciting cause. But after the initial damage, bacteria and yeast can become the bigger danger. Not only that, he may also be suffering from kidney damage due to accumulations of inflammatory materiel from those uncontrolled ear infections.

Have I made a case for taking this kitty to the doctor immediately? Treatment may require anesthesia to remove all that nasty discharge. Microscopic evaluations plus cultures will be useful. Injectable and oral antibiotics may also help. This sounds like a lot—it has to be to get this boy back to the health he deserves. Please don't wait any longer.

Ear Mites

Nasty little creatures drive cats crazy. Injections from your veterinarian are easier for you and your cat than pet store ear drops.

QUESTION:

We have three cats at our house and all of them are scratching their ears. This has been going on for a long time. We took them to the doctor and she said that she saw ear mites. She even showed them to my kids and me in the microscope. The doctor said that she could give the cats injections to get rid of the mites, but with three of them, I picked up ear drops at the pet store instead. It's much cheaper. The problem is that the cats fight with me every time I try to put the ear drops in. How can I make them hold still?

DR. NICHOL:

You have two common problems. One is ear mites and the other is cats who won't hold still. Try to see it from a cat's point of view. There are these actively running and scurrying insects in your head driving you crazy. Then this person shows up and tries to wrestle you down and squirt medicine in—that by the way irritates the heck out of the ear tissue. (They don't tell you that on the label.) Cats are no dummies. If they already hurt, they have no interest in adding to their pain. But don't lose faith. Your cats will love you again.

First, I will address the question of expense. As you continue your well-intentioned treatment attempts at home, the ears get worse. Not only are the ear mites (*Otobious Megnini*—the dreaded spinose ear tick) multiplying, bacterial infection is also on the rise. That's because the mites are damaging the walls of the cats' ear canals and bacteria are setting up housekeeping. The longer the ears mites stay, the worse the secondary infection. By the time you finally surrender to the attack of the ear mites, your cats and their health will be paying for it. When you take them back to the veterinarian for treatment, you will pay a bigger price because by then they will need not just the injections for the mites but treatment for their ear infections, too.

Your second concern needs to be your relationship with your cats. If you treasure the trust you have with those pets, make it easy for them. The injection, called Ivermectin, is essentially painless. Bring them in together, then return for a repeat in two to three weeks. Then you are done and your cats will thank you. They will also act more civilized if they don't have bugs in their heads.

Head Shaking in Cats Can Mean Foxtails in the Ear

A sudden onset suggests a grass awn (foxtail). Have it checked out soon.

QUESTION:

I have a head problem with Schnapps. Schnapps is our cat and she is a female. All of a sudden two days ago she's been leaning her head to the right. Sometimes she sort of shakes her head, too. She seems OK in

other ways. What's wrong with Schnapps? Will this problem go away by itself?

DR. NICHOL:

I'm glad you are asking for advice on Schnapps's problem. While it will not go away by itself, it also may not be serious.

There are a few possible causes for Schnapps's head tilt. Middle- and inner-ear infections can do it as well as dental disease. Even a brain tumor is a possibility. But considering that it came on suddenly and that she is doing well in other respects, I would suspect first that Schnapps has a foxtail awn stuck in her ear canal.

What is a foxtail awn, you ask? Foxtail is an aggressive weed that grows in fields and in many yards. The branches of the weed look like the bushy tail of a fox—hence the name. Stuck to the shaft of the branches are dozens of awns that break loose and blow around the yard. The awns are shaped like the birdie used in the game of badminton. They are pointed at the tip. "Feathers" project away from the tip. Each of the feathers has tiny barbs like a fish hook. If you have weeds in your yard, you have probably found foxtail awns stuck in your socks after walking through the weeds. As your ankle and your socks move, the foxtail migrates further and further into your sock until it starts to rub your skin. The more you walk with a foxtail stuck in your sock, the worse it bugs you. That is exactly what is happening in Schnapps's ear. A foxtail has found its way to the opening of her ear canal and, as she moves, it works its way further in. No wonder her ear is bothering her.

What poor Schnapps needs is to have the foxtail awn removed using instruments called an otoscope and an alligator forcep. Most cats hold still for the removal of foreign material like this. If she gets wild on her doctor, Schnapps may need to be sedated.

The question I often get at this point is "Won't it just come out by itself?" This almost never happens. Because of the shape of the awns and the barbs on their feathers, they tend to just keep moving in. So if you don't get it removed soon, it can continue its movement until it reaches Schnapps's eardrum, penetrates it, and possibly continues into her brain. That is the worst part of the problem. Foxtail awns have been found in every part of the anatomy of dogs and cats. Not only have they been found in brains, but spinal cords, livers, lungs, you name it. They can travel anywhere in the body if given enough time. So the moral of the story is: Get this type of problem managed fast to avoid advanced foxtail migration.

Sores on the Ears of White Cats

Lacking protective dark skin pigment, white cats are vulnerable to skin cancer.

QUESTION:

Our cat is 8 years old and we've noticed that he has little red sores on each of his ears. They've been there for a few weeks and they don't seem to heal. I don't know if it's important but Bronson is a white cat and he is outside most of the time. Do you think this is a problem?

DR. NICHOL:

Yes, it is important. It is likely that Bronson has a malignant skin cancer called squamous cell carcinoma. This form of skin cancer is quite common in people as well as critters living at high elevations.

What can we do for Bronson? Since the problem sounds like it's in its early stages, the simplest treatment would be amputation of his earflaps. Since squamous-cell carcinoma does not spread to other parts of the body, surgery should be curative. On the other hand, if the lesions are still tiny, he can keep his earflaps by having them treated with radiation instead. So the news is actually pretty good. But you may object to the idea of amputation of Bronson's earflaps, knowing that his friends will start calling him "E.T."

Eyes

■ ■

Eye and Nose Discharge

Infectious upper respiratory diseases can linger and run rampant in multiple-cat households.

QUESTION:

I have a litter of white kittens who are approximately 3 months old, plus six cats. They have never been outside, but they have developed a discharge from their eyes and scabs around their noses. Only two of them are infected. They have not had any shots as of yet. Their behavior has not changed, and they run and play and eat really well. And now another cat is getting the same symptoms. I am concerned it might be distemper, even though they never go outside.

DR. NICHOL:

I think I can help you with your herd health problem. Herd health? A herd of cats? Sounds absurd, doesn't it? In a way, it is. Think about dogs running in a pack or birds on the wing in a flock or livestock being moved as a herd. But cats don't behave that way, do they? The reason that cats don't exhibit group behavior is that unlike most other species, cats are not community animals. So when they are kept in a group such as yours, they are in an unnatural living arrangement. The result is stress that, in the case of your cats, shows up as physical disease.

This is not to say that cats kept alone live more meaningful lives. For indoor cats to have symptoms of infectious disease, someone sometime brought it into the group from the outside. That someone has had a smoldering infection for a while—what's called a carrier state. No symptoms, no discharge, no scabs. Then along comes a litter of vulnerable kittens and one after the other they start to get sick.

Now that you understand the problem, let's help your kitties out of this mess. The infectious cause of the upper respiratory symptoms is likely to be a virus called feline viral rhinotracheitis. Other complicating organisms may include calici virus, chlamydia, and bacteria. Drugs like antibiotics can be helpful in controlling the bacteria (the "groupies" of upper respiratory infections of cats). But for the most part, your best defense will be good nursing care, like keeping their little noses free of snot, and providing ginger ale and videos until they feel well enough to go back to school. In other words, it has to run its course.

I know I make it sound easy—just wait it out. The truth is that if you continue with this crowded living arrangement, you may never be rid of it. I mean *never*—remember the carrier state in a herd of cats? So the morale of the story is: Find homes for all of the kittens where they will each be the only pet. Next, give your adult cats more space—that is, keep only one indoors. The forces of nature are at odds with your cat management. And, you know that it's not nice to fool Mother Nature.

The Third Eyelid

Third eyelids can be visible with stress, infection, or foreign material. A good exam is important and essential.

QUESTION:

I must say that I am very worried about my Maine Coon kitten. This morning, when we woke up, we found that one of her eyes had an off-white coating on most of the eye. It doesn't seem to bother him (he's not scratching at it or grooming it or anything else) but it really worries me. It looks like the stuff that is usually in the inner corner of his eye. My daughter has said that when other cats she has had developed this condition, they died. Can you tell me what causes this condition, and what can or should be done about it?

DR. NICHOL:

I'm glad you and your daughter have taken this cat's symptoms seriously. Here is the long and short of this situation: What you describe is called a protracted third eyelid. The third eyelid is actually a normal structure that all cats and dogs have. It also goes by the name nictitans or nictitating membrane. What's important about it is its protective function. On the back side of the third eyelid is a patch of lymph tissue like a mini lymph node; thus, it helps clean up infections and debris. In addition, the third eyelid can easily slide up over the entire cornea (the clear front part of the eye). Most people never notice that their pets even own such equipment because the third eyelid normally sits tucked neatly in the inside corner of the eye. In this position it can move up to shield the eye from injury or help heal it if it gets injured. Pretty nifty. Too bad we don't have them. If you look closely at the inside corner of your eyes, you will see a small pink tissue that is an evolutionary vestige of a third eyelid. It's all we have left of ours. Maybe we humans have just gotten too good for such things. Oh, how I yearn for simpler times. . . .

Enough nostalgia; back to your question. What does it mean when you actually notice that your cat has a third eyelid? If it's visible on only one side, it suggests an infection or injury to that eye only. On the other hand, if both third eyelids are protracted, we need to be concerned about internal disease. We call it a sign of systemic illness because a disease in some other part of the body is responsible for the symptom. Diseases that can cause protracted third eyelids in cats include any physical or emotional stress as well as severe problems like feline leukemia and feline infectious peritonitis (FIP) infections. The entire list of possibilities would be quite long. Suffice it to say that any stress can do it.

Here is my advice: Have your daughter take this kitty to a veterinarian with lots of experience with cats. A thorough physical exam alone could answer the question. If not, screening lab work like a blood count, chemistry panel, and urinalysis are in order to look for indicators of internal disease. In addition, testing for leukemia virus is essential. The last big concern, FIP virus, can be investigated if physical signs and initial lab work suggest it.

So, how sick is this kitty? The truth is that without a good exam and lab work, I can only guess. Her problem may be as simple as a minor stress or as severe as a terminal illness. But like any possibly serious disease, early diagnosis and treatment are your best hope. Good luck.

Uneven Pupils

It may be normal, or maybe not. Get a good physical exam.

QUESTION:

We have recently acquired a new cat to our household. She is an odd-eyed white. The pupil in the blue eye is always larger than the pupil in the yellow eye. Is this normal? She seems to be in good health otherwise.

DR. NICHOL:

Congratulations on your new kitty. You were smart to examine her carefully. Actually there are lots of white cats with eyes of different colors. Many with one or both blue eyes are deaf. That part's really OK. But differing pupil size (called anisocoria) may or may not be normal. There could be several possible causes including cancer, glaucoma, infections, or nerve damage.

This girl needs a thorough physical exam. It should include an evaluation of the interior of her eyes using an ophthalmascope as well as measurements of the pressures inside her eyes. These procedures plus a few neurologic tests will hopefully show negative for disease. Last, ask for a feline leukemia test. This potentially fatal infection can cause spastic pupil syndrome. (This sounds strangely like descriptions of me in grade school.) The blood test is fast and reliable.

I know it sounds grim but the truth is that most cats with anisocoria are actually fine—what we call a variant of normal. But don't gamble. Your girl sounds special. Get her checked out for your peace of mind.

Eye Discharge

Don't goof around at home. See the doctor fast.

QUESTION:

I just noticed today that my cat's eyes were tearing and one was infected with green pus. Is there any way I can treat her myself? She is kept indoors.

DR. NICHOL:

Please do *not* monkey around with eye disease. Discharge coming from just one eye suggests a possible injury to that eye. Without thorough diagnosis and appropriate treatment, she could end up with big-time pain and blindness. Go directly to the nearest veterinarian. Do not pass "Go." Do not collect $200.

Feeding and Nutrition

Milk for Cats

Kitties love milk—but it's not part of a balanced diet, unless you're a calf.

QUESTION:

I am in first grade and have an assignment that is asking why cats like milk. Why do they like milk?

DR. NICHOL:

Cats enjoy milk for the same reasons people do: It tastes great. That's because it has plenty of animal fat and protein. Cow's milk makes a fine diet for baby cows—not really for cats. The best thing to feed a cat is cat food. But you like milk and so does your cat. So I think you can each have some—just don't let it spoil your appetite for your real dinner.

Varying the Diet—Changing Brands of Pet Food

Variety is the spice of life, but cats can get gas and diarrhea. Pick a good diet and stay the course.

QUESTION:

I live alone and my cat is my constant companion. I know I spoil her, but I can't help it. She's 4 years old and I have noticed that she seems to grow tired of a particular food after a while. So, like the doting cat mother I am, I give her something different. The problem is that I often find loose or fluid stool in her litter pan. She smells gassy, too. What can I do?

Dr. Nichol:

What you are describing is something very familiar to most of us cat owners. They can be finicky. But you can allow your kitty to be fussy and still enjoy good health.

To manage this problem, you need to first understand that the stomach and intestinal tract of cats is truly a creature of habit. In other words, most cats do best eating the same diet every day, long term. With frequent changes in the diet, the intestine has to change the way it manages the differences in fiber, proteins, and fat. Bloating with gas and diarrhea can result. When these problems occur, you are also likely to notice your cat making urgent, more frequent trips to the litter pan. This problem is not only unpleasant for you, but uncomfortable for your cat.

The best prevention for the loose stool and gas problem is to use the same diet. Your best choice is one of the higher fiber cat foods. While not all cats have this problem with changes in diet, those who do usually need more fiber. Ask your veterinarian for a recommended diet. Prescription diet r/d is a good choice.

What about the enjoyment? Use cat treats. Be sure to limit your kitty to two per day. Treat her like a child (our pets are really just furry children anyway). Give her one cat treat after she finishes her breakfast and another after dinner. If you stick to that structure, she'll go along, too.

Finicky Eaters

What's good, what's junk, why it matters.

Question:

For most of my cat's 12 years she would only eat canned food. She got cat acne and our vet suggested it was due to the wet food. We have tried many varieties of semi-moist and dry foods and she seems to hate them all. She seems to always be hungry, yet she often won't eat the food we give her. Recently I noticed her eating our dog's food quite often. As the cat has lost weight, I am worried about her.

Dr. Nichol:

Your cat's quirky appetite isn't unusual. Aging cats get so set in their ways that some would prefer a hunger strike to following their doctor's diet advice. So let's accept realities. If this girl forgets to clean those sticky bits of canned food off her chin, then I say let's wipe her face for her. I do it for my kids everyday. (Shucks, I wipe food off my own chin, too.) A clean, dry chin should prevent the feline acne that prompted the diet change in the first place.

So, how about canned food? Like all types of pet food, there are excellent canned diets on the shelf right next to the bargain-priced junk. Get the good stuff like Science Diet or Iams. But also be sure she isn't eating poorly and losing weight because of dental infections, organ failure, or cancer. If your feline senior citizen hasn't had a thorough exam in the past six months, she may have serious reasons for failing to eat. Ask your veterinarian for a geriatric lab and X-ray profile. If we catch age-related problems early, we can extend the excellent quality of life that your loving care has always given her.

Cats are special creatures, aren't they? It's really true that their behavior is fundamentally different from dogs and humans. My cat Raoul has seen me through good times and bad over our 15 years together. I love him intensely. He doesn't spend his life trying to please me, but he's always my friend.

Poor Eaters: When Cats Lose Their Appetite

Elderly cats who fail to eat may have serious illness. But we can help many.

Question:

We have a 20-year-old female cat. She will not eat canned cat food from the pet stores. I have tried many brands, but she will go many days before finally eating a little. My wife wanted to know if there are any recipes available she could cook up that our cat might eat. We are worried she is not getting enough food.

DR. NICHOL:

Thanks for writing. You are right to be concerned, but please do not try to manage your feline senior citizen's poor appetite by trying new foods. What is truly important is to understand *why* she is not eating. Possible reasons in a 20-year-old cat include painful infected teeth, organ failure, and cancer. Frankly, this mature lady is on borrowed time. There is much wear and tear by age 20. That does not mean she should be written off. There may be a few good miles left for you to share. But be careful. If you allow the cause of her poor appetite to continue without treatment, she is likely to crash suddenly.

Get this girl the care she needs. Have her examined soon. Get a thorough geriatric lab screen so her doctor can find the age-related problems that can be managed. Do whatever it takes so you three can enjoy those golden years. It sounds like she is well loved.

Overeating

Most hungry, overweight cats are just bored.

QUESTION:

My 8-year-old cat, Nelson, was placed on IVD special diet three years ago. I have noticed that giving him the same measured amounts of food have recently caused him to gain weight. He always acts famished, so I am reluctant to reduce the amount. Being a housecat, he is inactive and cannot burn off the calories. Can you recommend another limited diet plan product for him to try? He is my firstborn, after all, and I want to keep him around at least another eight years.

DR. NICHOL:

Does Nelson threaten you with action from Animal Humane? Does he stagger into the room with the back of his paw against his forehead and flop unconsciously at your feet—even though he can barely fit through the door? I think I know this guy. I've met him a thousand times.

I know how you feel about Nelson. My cat Raoul always insists that he's never been fed. Cats are such con artists. The only viable treatment is finding this bored teenager whole-some after-school activities. If he already owns a cat tree with feathers-on-a-stick toys attached, get him a window-mounted birdhouse or a fish tank. If his gluttony continues to haunt your relationship, I suggest offering raw carrot wheels. If he won't eat them, maybe he'll chase them and burn off a little fat.

How Much to Feed

Being overweight is unhealthy. Here's how to get it right.

QUESTION:

How much should I feed my cat? I thought I was doing the right thing by following the recommendations on the bag, but when I took Shalako for his shots, he weighed over 12 pounds. Now I feel guilty that he may not get old because his doctor said that overweight cats usual-ly don't. How much is the right amount?

DR. NICHOL:

This is a very good question. Please don't feel guilty for trying to do the right thing for Shalako. There are many things in life that we cannot change. Be thankful that body weight is not one of them.

Your veterinarian is right. Extra weight puts extra strain on the heart, kidneys, and joints. In cats we have the added risk of a potentially fatal liver disease, too. So thin is in.

What's the right amount? Remember that pets are a lot like us in that they have differing individual needs. But the average adult cat does fine on a quarter cup of dry food morning and night. This amount should help Shalako maintain a weight of around $8\frac{1}{2}$ to $9\frac{1}{2}$ pounds. You say Shalako is just big-boned? Even a big-framed cat has no business weighing more than $10\frac{1}{2}$ pounds. Because Shalako is male, be sure to add some water to his dry food to help prevent crystals from forming in his bladder.

Here is how I determine if a pet's weight is healthy. With the pet standing, feel for the ribs with your fingertips. If you can count the ribs with your fingers, but you cannot see the ribs individually, that critter is about right. If you can't find the ribs with your fingers, your pet needs to lose weight. Use the above feeding recommendations as a starting point. Then adjust the amount fed as needed.

So the last question is: Why did Shalako get fat following the manufacturer's advice? Shouldn't they know best how to feed their diet? The answer is that the manufacturer's advice is based on cats and dogs who live in research colonies—a very different life than your pets. Pet food companies are also in the business of promoting pet food sales. Your veterinarian is in the business of promoting pet health.

What about Feeding Cats Corn?

Are you crazy? Dogs and cats don't eat corn in the wild. They need meat, right?

QUESTION:

Can animals, dogs and cats, digest corn? I know that in most cat/dog food the number-one ingredient is ground corn meal, or something like that. If they can't digest it, isn't most of the food you feed your dog or cat just "running though them"?

DR. NICHOL:

Don't you know that reading food labels can be dangerous to your health? Why, you can become anxious and stressed. Let me help both you and your pets to live a lot longer.

Corn is fine. Heresy you say? Aren't cats and dogs carnivores? Aren't they supposed to stealthily track cute woodland vegetarian creatures, pounce on them, and then rip them to pieces? Sure they are. So, why are vegetables in the diet of your carnivorous pets? Because when inveterate predators like our pets eat their prey, they eat *all* of their prey. That means the hair, bone, organs, intestinal contents, and a bit of meat (muscle). In other words, they get a balanced diet in the wild by eating what their food ate—vegetation.

Pet food labels. Don't get too excited. Simply understand that ingredients and guaranteed analyses are regulated by laws that are riddled with loopholes and nuance. There is really no way for you to know the true digestibility or nutritional value of your pets' food by reading the container—except for one clue: price.

During my years in practice I have seen the physical results of every type of pet food. The good stuff costs more, but results in healthier haircoats and more active immune systems. Your pets will feel better. It's clear from your letter that you want the best for them. But you won't get what you don't pay for. Spend a couple of extra bucks and give your pets the best.

Cheap Pet Food Is No Bargain

Lower-priced diets boast comparisons to the better brands, but you won't get what you don't pay for.

QUESTION:

I read an article recently in <u>Consumer Reports</u> that said some of the lower-priced pet foods are a much better deal than food like Science Diet because the ingredients are just as good but the price is much

lower. But you've said that the premium brands are better. Somebody doesn't have their story straight.

Dr. Nichol:

You're not the first person to raise this point. In fact, Hills Pet Products, makers of Science Diet and Health Blend diets, took issue directly with *Consumer Reports* over their faulty methods of analysis. The magazine has written an apology to Hills stating that they will redo the analysis more thoroughly and reprint their findings.

It turns out that *Consumer Reports* got into this mess for the same reason many pet owners do: They believed the labels on the lower-priced foods. Isn't it illegal to lie on the package, you ask? Well, in the strictest sense they are not lying. By the use of parentheses and commas, the order in which ingredients are listed, and the loophole of allowing some ingredient names to encompass many different sources of nutrition, a pet food company can make its product look pretty good. Unfortunately for many pets, the real differences are striking. To make the point, shoe leather has been analyzed for its protein content. The results are around 22 percent—roughly comparable to many pet foods. Too bad you can't recycle your old shoes, handbags, and gloves by feeding them to your pets.

I will conclude my response to poor-quality diets by recounting my observations of the health of the pets I examine and treat on a daily basis. Cheap food, no matter how low the price, results in poor haircoats, large volumes of soft stool (lots more to clean up), poor weight, and diminished defenses against disease. In addition, the high salt content and excessive quantities of poor digestibility protein adds to the risk of kidney failure as these bargain-fed pets age. As the old saw goes: The bitterness of poor quality is remembered long after the sweetness of low price is forgotten. Put differently: You don't get what you don't pay for.

Dogs Eating Cat Food and Cats Eating Dog Food

Cats and dogs are different species with very different needs. Poor health can result from the wrong diet.

QUESTION:

Our 8-month-old Pomeranian–Dachshund sure enjoys eating the cat food! (Although the cat doesn't appreciate it much.) Is this a bad thing? Also, the cat kinda digs the dog food once in a while. What do you think?

DR. NICHOL:

This reminds me of how much our pets resemble our children. Regardless of how well intentioned our efforts to give them what is right, they want the opposite. It's tempting to just let it go. After all, pet food tends to look the same anyway, right?

Well, I'm glad you asked. There are significant nutritional differences between cat and dog foods and for good reasons. For starters, the physiology of cats requires that their bodies function at a more acid pH. This necessitates a diet much higher in protein. They also need more of the amino acid taurine. Insufficient levels of taurine result in a terminal heart condition called dilated cardiomyopathy. So for a cat who eats a diet heavy on dog food, there will be serious deficiencies.

How about a dog eating cat food? Not only do dogs need less protein, they pay a big price if they get too much. By far the most common organ failure disease in older dogs is kidney failure. One big cause for this is, you guessed it, excessive protein in their diets.

So, the last question has to be: How do you fight this battle and win? First I'll tell you what does *not* work. Do not sit them down and have a heart to heart. Explaining that these species-specific diets are for their own good won't work on your pets anymore than on your kids. ("Yeah right, Dad." No respect.)

Also forget the idea of supervising them while they eat. When it comes to food, pets are masters of deceit and diversion. Your only hope is to feed all adult pets twice daily. Give each pet his or her own measured amount of food in his or her very own bowl—and here's the most important part—in an isolated separate room with the door closed. When everyone is finished eating, you pick up the bowls and mealtime is over.

I know I speak of our pets as though they are devious creatures who love us unconditionally. But they know I'm right, don't they? Naw. But they will thank me later.

Designer Pet Foods and High Price

If the ingredients match and the analysis looks as good, why pay more? Because you won't get what you don't pay for.

QUESTION:

I read an article in last week's paper that got me to thinking about how much money I spend feeding my animals. The article talked about "designer" pet foods and said that regular food like Dog Chow was just as good, but that a lot of people buy the pricier food because it's recommended by their vet. Isn't it really all the same?

DR. NICHOL:

I wish more people asked this question. There is an enormous number of pet foods available nowadays. Whether you buy it in the supermarket, pet supply store, veterinary hospital, or health food store, there are way too many choices. With our lives in America getting as complicated and busy as they are, it should be a lot simpler. I will make it simple for you now.

The first point is the type of food. In other words, should you feed hard dry, canned, or the semi-moist stuff that comes in the cellophane packages? The answer to that, unless you have been given a medical reason, is never feed anything but hard dry food. It's healthier for the teeth and gums than soft food and it's much cheaper to feed. If you need convincing, note that dry food is about 13-percent moisture (water) while canned food is 75-percent moisture. Semi-moist is somewhere between them. Add to that the additional cost of packaging (about 25 cents for the can itself) and you begin to see that dry is the only way to go. For those pets who refuse dry food, I would forget lecturing them on the importance of healthy teeth. Kids these days never listen anyway. They got no respect.

What about senior, less active, and light diets? While there are pets who need a special food for weight loss or for management of an age-related problem, the diets available at the grocery or pet supply store are only slightly different from the regular stuff. Only the prescription foods that your veterinarian has are going to make a significant difference for pets who are overweight or geriatric. So what is left is regular dry pet food—in a million different brands and prices.

Now, the informed pet lover feels an obligation to read the ingredients and nutritional analysis on the bag and compare brands. This would seem to make sense, but the pet food manufacturers are way ahead of you. They know that with sleight of hand they can word their list of ingredients to appear to outclass the others *and* beat the competition on price. If that weren't enough, they also provide you the nutritional analysis, you know, the percent of protein, carbohydrates—everything a healthy pet needs in the greatest quantity possible, right? It's enough to give a normal person a headache.

Here's how it works. If you are a cheap pet food company bent on making a quick buck, you can design an impressive label listing great ingredients and high percentages of protein. Then you find the cheapest sources possible. Does it matter to the health of pets? You bet it does. In our hospital we see pets fed every diet you've ever heard of and many whose names we hear only once. Poor-quality food results in rough haircoats, soft stools, poor exercise tolerance, and sometimes the inability to maintain normal weight. On the other hand, the genuinely excellent diets not only prevent these problems, these pets also stay energetic much later in their lives. They just seem to feel better.

So, how do you know which foods are worth feeding and which are just a lot of hype? Price. It's really that simple. If a diet is really highly digestible with truly high-quality nutrients, it cannot be possible to produce it at a bargain price. You will not get what you don't pay for. Who can afford the highest priced food? Anybody—here's why. One way to make a seemingly good-quality pet food at a low price is to add fillers like wheat hulls. The bag really weighs what it says—but it's not really all food. Since the body knows how much bioavailable calories it needs, your pet will require a lot more volume just to get the necessary calories. So if she's eating more volume, you're going to buy food much more often than if you fed the good stuff. The bottom line is that your expenses for pet food will be about the same over the long term whether you feed higher-priced excellent food or cheaper food that claims to be just as good. And, while your long-term cost is about the same, the health of your pets will be much better if you choose higher-quality food. So cheap is not better. Better is better. You really cannot get the best for less. The pet food business is really competitive. If the makers of the better diets could produce their foods for less money, they would.

One last point: With high levels of filler in cheap food, there is a lot more waste—you know, that nasty stuff you shovel up in the yard or litter pan. If you are the pooper scooper at your house, better pet food will improve your quality of life, too.

Grooming and Skin Care

Skunked Pets

Tomato juice or a new mixture can make a pet worth having back in the county.

Question:

Do you have any suggestions on how to deodorize a skunked pet?

Dr. Nichol:

I hate it when that happens. There are a few products on the shelves of pet supply stores that claim effectiveness for pets who have tangled with the business end of a skunk. But the best treatment still seems to be tomato juice.

Start by bathing your cat (don't do it like a cat or hair will stick to your tongue). Next, plug the drain in the sink and sponge tomato juice onto every square inch of your kitty, allowing him or her to soak for a good 15 minutes before rinsing. Do not shampoo after the tomato juice.

Don't expect this approach to totally eliminate the odor, but you will at least be able to share the same county. Lastly, your pet won't "learn a lesson." Cats already know everything and dogs don't care.

But wait, there's more. Don't touch that dial. A new and exciting way to deskunk your skunked pet. Paul Krebaum, a chemist at Molex, Inc., advises: one quart 3-percent hydrogen peroxide, one-quarter cup baking soda, one teaspoon liquid soap. Make the solution fresh just before use. Rinse the pet with tap water after soaking. I'm so excited I just can't wait for one of my pets to give me a chance to give it a try.

Haircuts

Shorter hair is easier to manage, but be careful to keep the skin protected.

QUESTION:

I have a 22-pound cat with very long fur. He gets ticks and thorns, etc., caught in his fur every day. I brush him the best I can, but he still accumulates debris and pests when he goes outside. My question is, could I shave off his fur?

DR. NICHOL:

Yes, it's a great idea to give this boy a haircut. Be sure that it is no shorter than one-half inch or his skin may be unprotected. If you make him look like a Marine recruit, he will not only be fat, but sunburned—and quite mad.

Soft Paws Instead of Declawing

These glue-on nail covers are a reasonable alternative, but they need to be maintained.

QUESTION:

My husband wants me to declaw my 7-month-old kitten and I don't want to do it. There are supposed to be some kind of plastic nails to place over their nails. What are they called and where do I find them? HELP!

DR. NICHOL:

I share your apprehension about declawing. Who wants part of their cat's God-given anatomy in the trashcan if there's an alternative? Not me. I have *all* of my claws.

For those unfamiliar with the onychectomy (spiffy name for declawing), the surgery amounts to removal of the end of the toe including the nail. In other words, we separate the last joint of each toe, then use surgical glue to close the wound in the skin. A new technique utilizes laser surgery, but it's expensive and the equipment is largely unavailable. While it sounds tough on the kitty, pain medications help a lot and recovery would be quick with a youngster like yours. But I still wouldn't do it unless your indoor kitten is shredding your furniture or your body.

There is an alternative: Soft Paws. This nifty product includes individual silicon rubber nail coverings. The cat's nails are trimmed, a drop of special glue is applied, and the nail covering is fitted over each of your cat's claws. They even come in colors so your cat can make a fashion statement—just like you. Isn't that easy? Yes, but the nails will grow and sometimes the Soft Paws fall off, so you'll have to fiddle with these for a lifetime. I've found most cats to be a bit fussy about their feet, which can make the whole exercise a bit arduous. You can have your veterinarian order them and do it all for you or you can buy them at a pet supply store and do it yourself. Simply a must for all stylin' cats.

Heart and Breathing

Breathing Difficulty

Persian cats can have a simple surgery to correct their narrow nostrils.

Question:

We have three Persian cats. Two are just fine, but one of them (2 years old) has trouble breathing. Her nostrils are very narrow. Can anything be done to help her breathe a little easier? I thought maybe tubes can be inserted.

Dr. Nichol:

This kitty has stenotic nares; it's as though her nose is being pinched. Persian cats have pushed-in faces that, in some cases, make the sides of the nostrils cave-in on themselves. You are right about it being difficult for her to breathe. It's especially tough for her when she runs, because the faster she tries to get air into her lungs, the more those nostrils collapse. If she needed to move really fast, being unable to get enough air could cause her to panic. She needs help.

The good news is that there's a pretty simple fix. A wedge-shaped piece of tissue from the side of each nostril can be surgically removed. Stitching the edges of the nostril across the gap created by the missing wedge will allow those nostrils to permanently stay open big enough for her to breathe normally. But while it's a basically straightforward procedure, not every veterinarian will want to handle it. Those of us who have helped brachycephalic (pushed-in faced) dogs like Pugs and Pekingnese could do an artful job. Cats, in general, are known for their vanity. But Persian cats, well, they're like royalty. For her it better be a purrr-fect nose job. But tubes? No way. Only punk cats have tubes in their noses.

Heart Disease

Cardiomyopathy can cause blood clots. Severe pain and paralysis can be debilitating.

QUESTION:

My cat has just had his second thromboembolism. My vet has treated him with heparin. Does he need anything else?

DR. NICHOL:

This is a tough problem. The blood clots in your cat are caused by a heart disease called cardiomyopathy. It is a severely debilitating condition of the heart muscle. Sludging of the blood in the left atrium of the heart leads to clots that can stop blood flow—most often to the rear legs. It's extremely painful.

Depending on your cat's ECG, cardiac drugs may be needed. Anticoagulant "blood-thinners" like heparin and Warfarin are often helpful. But these are risky. Warfarin is the active ingredient in rodent poisons. It must be dosed and monitored carefully. Aspirin, on the other hand, may be sufficient—and it's much safer.

Your cat's doctor may also prescribe blood pressure medication. These are hard cases. The long-term prognosis for your kitty is not great. Enjoy every day with this boy.

Coughing Cats

Asthma is common in cats, but it's not the only cause of coughing.

QUESTION:

Hunter is my 6-year-old kitty and she's been coughing lately. I take really good care of her and she stays inside all of the time. She eats fine and plays. Could Hunter have asthma?

DR. NICHOL:

Yes, she could, but it's not the only possibility. I know I'm starting to sound like a broken record, but before you assume anything, get Hunter thoroughly checked out. Other causes could include pneumonia, FIP, heart failure, heartworm infection, or even foreign materiel in her airways or lungs. A clear diagnosis is needed.

I would start with a good exam. Of course the most important part of it is listening to Hunter's chest. What kind of lung sounds does she have? Is there a nice quiet movement of air or harsh dry sounds, wet sounds, or noise on only one side? What about a heart murmur? Armed with these answers, we will take chest X-rays next. Lung tissues can have many different appearances on X-ray. Asthma cases look pretty typical. With asthma, we expect only slightly dry sounds, with the chest X-rays confirming our suspicion.

Can we help Hunter feel better and stop coughing? Feline asthma usually responds well to treatment. There are a few medications that work well in individual kitties, so we can do what we call therapeutic trials to see what will help. Many cats do best on prednisone, a corticosteroid. Not only is it reliable but cats handle it safely long term. Most important, *no smoking*.

Intestinal and Stomach Problems

Vomiting

Never considered normal, it occurs more often over time. Early diagnosis and treatment prevent bigger trouble later.

QUESTION:

Our 14-year-old male cat seems to be in good health and has a good appetite, but vomits almost daily. I changed his diet to Science Diet Hairball Control for Adult Cats. I took him off wet food. That has not stopped the problem.

DR. NICHOL:

This is miserable for your boy. Every time he vomits, stomach acid is forced into his lower esophagus, causing weight loss and more pain for this poor little guy. Over time his chronic vomiting will occur with increasing frequency. By the time it's happening daily, we know there's more to it than just hairballs.

So, let's get started on finding the cause. Following a thorough physical exam, he needs a complete blood, stool, and urine workup plus abdominal X-rays to check for problems like kidney, thyroid, and liver diseases as well as some cancers. If he clears these hurdles, we're going to need information taken directly from the site of his vomiting: the inner walls of the stomach and small intestine.

Surgery? Naw, we're much too high tech for that. Using a long snake-like instrument called an endoscope, we can see the interior of his esophagus, stomach, and upper intestines. More important, we can take a dozen or more tiny scraps of tissue for biopsy while we're in there.

Should vomiting be this complicated? Your cat's body is sending strong signals that there are serious problems. This little guy feels rotten. Diet changes won't do the job. But I can tell you that most persistently puking pussycats are manageable with medications for problems ranging from parasites and chronic inflammatory disorders to intestinal malignancies. But the longer you delay, the more deeply entrenched his problems will be. Get going now.

Tapeworms

Simple to kill, tapeworms are carried by fleas or rodents. Fleas are much worse than tapeworms. Declare war on fleas. Careful with the chinchilla.

QUESTION:

I was recently adopted by a young, female, seal point Siamese who has tapeworms. I understand that tapeworms come from fleas. I didn't see any fleas on her. Now that I have given her the medication, how long should I expect it to take for the worms to go away? Are they contagious to other animals or even humans? I also have a chinchilla, which I am worried about getting the worms, since my cat likes to antagonize the chinchilla by sticking her paws and tail in the cage. Are there any other things I should do to insure the demise of these creatures?

DR. NICHOL:

Tapeworms are pretty creepy, aren't they? Let's start with a few fun facts. Tapeworms are made up of a series of segments that are each nearly complete parasites unto themselves. As the segments mature in the intestine, they fall off and show up on the fur around the rear end of the pet or in the stool. The segments contain eggs. But tapeworms cannot be passed directly from one critter to another by simply being swallowed. An intermediate host is needed. This creature eats the eggs and allows the development of a larva inside its body. When the real victim eats this middleman, she gets the worms themselves.

So the plot thickens. We have two types of tapeworms in our part of the world. One has the flea as its intermediate host and the other requires the services of rodents like mice. If your cat or dog has fleas, he or she can get tapes. If you have a rodent eater, it can happen. Now the truth about tapeworms themselves: They are worth killing but they don't do much harm. They are not responsible for weight loss except in huge numbers. What's more important is the intermediate hosts. If it's rodents, toss a biscuit to that hunter or huntress and say "good job." But if your pet has fleas, you'd better declare war. Fleas are much more than a cause for itching. They can carry other serious diseases like plague. And don't take the cheap route and buy flea stuff off the shelf. See your veterinarian for the heavy artillery and win. Lastly, the tapeworm treatment: Droncit. It's a great drug. It does the job with only one dose. The chinchilla: Careful there. Your cat is doing more than playing. She's rodent hunting.

Eating Cat Litter Can Cause Intestinal Blockage

Avoid clumping litter for these cats. Pelleted newspaper litter is much safer if eaten.

QUESTION:

I hope you can help. My 4-year-old tabby is in the hospital for eating kitty litter. He got several blockages in his intestines. My question is, how do I keep him from doing it again?

DR. NICHOL:

This must be really hard for you. It's unpleasant for your cat to have surgery to remove this stuff. As much as we love our pets and care for them, it's too bad we can't teach them good sense. I've heard pet owners ask if a disaster like this will be a lesson, but our pets just don't make the connection.

In trying to prevent a recurrence, it would be useful to understand why your cat would eat litter in the first place. Could his diet be lacking? Is he getting enough to eat? Is he bored? The likely answer is boredom. In addition, it's possible that he has developed a compulsive habit of eating the stuff.

So here is my advice: Set up a permanent hobby or healthy athletic activity for this guy. Try any of these ideas or a combination of them. Buy a tall scratching post with two or three carpeted little houses. You can add a few feathers-on-a stick toys to it for him to bat at. Consider getting another cat as a playmate. Even a fish tank could work in that it would keep him occupied. These diversions will help, but I wouldn't stop there. Just in case this fellow thinks your brand of litter tastes yummy, change brands. Not being a connoisseur of cat litter myself, I can't say which brand tastes the worst, but there is one that won't clump together and block his intestines. It's called Yesterday's News because, you guessed it, it's recycled newspaper. We use it at our animal hospital. It's pelleted, but it softens up when it's wet. We've had no odor problems with it.

The specific type of litter to be avoided is clumping litter. While there has been no definitive study, there is anecdotal evidence that litters that stick together when wet in the pan do the same thing when they reach the fluid in the stomach and intestines—and it's normally plenty wet in there. Since the best prevention of urinary disease in cats includes access to fresh unused litter, I always recommend cheaper throw-away litters anyway. A small amount in each of several pans around the house makes it easy for a cat to urinate often and avoid bladder problems. Pelleted newspaper absorbs well and falls apart when wet.

Sorry your boy had to undergo surgery to survive his dietary indiscretion. But know that by bringing this issue to other cat lovers, you have helped keep other kitties off the surgery table. Thanks.

Diarrhea in Kittens

Parasites and diet are major factors. Get a stool exam, feed an excellent kitten food, and prevent dehydration.

QUESTION:

I rescued two abandoned kittens at my workplace one week ago. They are approximately 5 weeks old. One of them has bad diarrhea. I'm feeding them kitten biscuits, kitten tin food, and weetbix mushed up with milk. What should I do about the diarrhea? Should I take her off wet foods and only give her water and kitten biscuits?

DR. NICHOL:

You are smart to be concerned. Diarrhea should never be considered acceptable, especially in youngsters. Severe dehydration could be just around the corner. Kittens can die quickly.

The best diet for babies this size is a high-quality, moistened dry cat or kitten food. There is no need to add canned food, milk, or anything else for variety. The better diets are both complete and balanced. This means that if you add to it, you will throw it out of balance. Your well-intentioned attempt to improve on a good diet has actually reduced its value. So, in answer to your question, the diet may be a factor in the diarrhea. But there may be an even more important cause: parasites.

Take a fresh stool sample to the nearest veterinarian. Do not pass "Go." Do not collect $200. A microscopic exam will show any parasite eggs. The correct medications can be started right away and the diarrhea should resolve within one to two days. In the meantime, provide plenty of fresh water and coax a teaspoonful of Gatorade into this baby every few hours to avoid electrolyte depletion. If she stops eating or acts weak, get emergency help.

You have done a very fine thing to help these homeless babies. Once the diarrhea is under control and they are on a steady diet, you can assume them to be free of physical stress. Start vaccinations when they are well. A good age for the first in the distemper–upper respiratory series is 6 to 8 weeks. They will need a booster three weeks later; another, three weeks after that. Rabies vaccine can be given with the last booster. Thanks for caring. You are a gentle soul.

Vomiting and Poor Appetite in an Overweight Cat

Fatty liver disease occurs in fat cats. Any stress that makes them stop eating can throw a kitty into liver failure.

QUESTION:

I have an 11-year-old cat named Frank who recently started to vomit. He quit eating, too. He's always been kind of pudgy, but his doctor told me that being overweight may have caused him to get a sick liver. He's not doing very well. Can you help?

DR. NICHOL:

What you are describing in Frank is called feline hepatic lipidosis—or fatty liver disease. It's a real serious problem and Frank needs to start taking in food soon or he may die from this. I will explain.

Hepatic lipidosis, while not only seen in fat cats, is more common in cases of obesity. Often the problem starts with some minor cause of loss of appetite. But soon the body starts to shift its fat stores, the cat loses weight, and begins to vomit. The end result can be failure of Frank's liver and death.

To get a handle on this problem, Frank's doctor will need to follow blood tests with a biopsy of his liver. This is done with a high-safety general anesthetic allowing the doctor to take a small scrap of liver tissue for microscopic examination by a pathologist. Knowing that it is truly hepatic lipidosis allows the doctor to give the right medication. But the most important treatment for Frank will be implanting a tube into his stomach so that a liquid diet can be given three times per day for several weeks. This is done either through the nostril, or through the body wall using an endoscope (called a P.E.G. tube). Even if Frank is still overweight, he must take in nutrition or his liver will fail and you will lose him. Fortunately, these cases often do well if they are treated early. Prevention is the best medicine: Never allow a pet to become overweight. Any pet with a weight problem needs a veterinarian's advice on safe methods of managing it.

Cats Who Play with String— High-Risk Behavior

Yarn, string, fish line can move through the intestines lengthwise. Multiple saw holes result. String and yarn can kill.

QUESTION:

Last week I was playing with our cat Flossy. I was having her chase a length of yarn. Well, when I was looking the other way, she up and swallowed the yarn—about 18 inches of it. I brought her to the veterinarian and they tried to get her to vomit, but she wouldn't. Finally, they took the yarn out of her stomach with an endoscope. Why was it so important? Couldn't she have just passed it in her stool?

DR. NICHOL:

Maybe that would have happened. But what also can happen is that the yarn can move into the intestine lengthwise. As the peristaltic (milking) movements of the intestine try to move it along like food, the yarn can start to saw holes in the intestinal wall. These holes leak bacteria and fluid, causing septic peritonitis which can quickly lead to death.

Swallowing yarn or string sounds innocent, but often it is not. Flossy's doctor acted quickly. The endoscope was a great choice of instruments. It saved Flossy from having to undergo surgery. It is quick and risk free. Good doctor.

Feline Distemper

The hallmark signs are vomiting and diarrhea. It's highly infectious and deadly. But vaccination is safe and effective.

QUESTION:

Four months ago we had a young cat who started vomiting and having diarrhea. We took him to the doctor. He was hospitalized and treated. We know that everything possible was done for him, but we lost him. It broke our hearts. The doctor said that little Homer had feline distemper. We kept meaning to get him vaccinated, but never got around to it. We're finally ready to try again to get a new cat. Is our home safe for a baby kitten?

DR. NICHOL:

It is difficult to lose a young kitten like Homer. Kittens are so full of life's energy. We bond so strongly to them. I know you don't want to go through that again.

Feline distemper's real name is infectious feline pan-leukopenia. It is caused by a virus in the parvo virus family. This organism is closely related to the parvo virus that causes such horrible disease in unvaccinated dogs. In fact it is likely that the virus that infects dogs was actually a mutation from the feline panleukopenia virus. While vaccination in cats is effective at prevention, it must be given in a series of two to three injections *before* your new kitten is exposed.

Your home is safe for a new kitten if you have properly disinfected it since the loss of Homer. The virus can be a resistant organism, so I recommend the following: mix Clorox bleach and water in a dilution of 1 part Clorox to 30 parts water. Wash all areas that Homer was exposed to—most important, food and water bowls as well as his litter pan.

Anyplace where vomit or diarrhea occurred needs special attention. Next, take the new kitten to the doctor for a thorough physical exam *before* you take him or her home for the first time. Be sure the new baby is healthy and be sure that the first vaccination is given. Follow through on the series and I think everyone will be fine. Vaccination, by the way, needs to be started at age 6 to 8 weeks.

Constipation in Kittens

Know what to do and when.

QUESTION:

My son found a 6-week-old kitten. She has a healthy appetite, she drinks a few ounces of kitten milk a day, but she is constipated—she only moved her bowels three days ago. We tried to stimulate her anus with a wet tissue, but she still doesn't go. Please tell us what to do. Thanks.

DR. NICHOL:

What I'm about to tell you is something that gives most folks that pinched expression that tells me they want our staff to handle the chore for them: She needs an enema. Eeeeewwww!

If you're tough, you can easily do it at home. First, go to your local veterinary hospital and ask for a stool-softening enema containing dioctyl sodium succinate (DSS). They are simple to use. They come packaged in a soft, pliable plastic syringe. Just spread Vaseline generously on the nozzle and insert it into the kitten's rectum, then push the plunger. Do not stand directly behind the kitten as you do this. Put her in her litter pan right away and stand back. That's all there is to it. You are now an expert. Or maybe you're not. If not, take the kitten to the hospital and return in a couple of hours. Just don't brag about this to your friends. (**Caution:** Do not use phosphate enemas on cats—they will kill.)

Constipation in Adult Cats

Many older cats have recurring problems. Here are some short-term and some long-term solutions.

QUESTION:

I'm worried about my cat Scratchy. Lately he's been going back and forth to the litter box a lot. Sometimes he cries when he's in there. I've looked to see what he's done and I can tell that he's making a good amount of urine, but I haven't seen any bowel movements for a while. He's not eating very well either. What should I do?

DR. NICHOL:

I'm glad that you are concerned enough about Scratchy to check his litter pan so carefully. While most of us pet owners have a pretty good idea of how well our critters are eating, it makes a lot of sense to be aware of their stool and urine, too. Since our pets can't talk to let us know if they are feeling sick, we must be observant.

Scratchy is a constipated kitty. It may be an advanced problem for his appetite to be affected. If he has hard stool that has backed up through his entire colon (large intestine), he may need the help of his doctor. But you can try to manage it for him on your own—just don't let it get to the point where he completely stops eating.

For home management, you will need to administer enemas. That's right, this is rear-end stuff and I meant it when I said more than one enema. You can use the old-fashioned enema bag with soapy water, but unless your cat has nerves of steel, you are both likely to get very wet—or worse. Instead, get a syringe-type disposable enema with a liquid stool softener called dioctyl sodium succinate (DSS). To give the enema, have a willing assistant hold Scratchy on a table with one hand on each of his shoulders. It'll work best if your helper pushes down gently on his shoulders so that Scratchy is lying on his chest. Your job is to lubricate the nozzle of the enema, grasp Scratchy's tail at the base, and hold it straight up. Then slide the end of the enema into his rectum—all the way to the wide portion of the syringe. (If you don't get the liquid DSS as far into the cat's rectum as possible, you won't do much good.) Then depress the plunger on the syringe and let go of one very surprised cat. (Do you still want to try this at home?)

How well will this work? Depending on how much hard stool there is, it may need to be repeated several times per day over three to four days. On the other hand, if the constipation is not severe, only one or two enemas may be enough.

As much as relieving a cat's constipation is really pretty straightforward, the bigger issue is avoiding a repeat performance. Some causes include diet changes, hair swallowed from grooming, chronic intestinal disorders, and old age. Here, too, you can try prevention at home. Oral lubricants like Laxatone or Petromalt are good, but messy. You can try adding

Metamucil to his food, but many cats would rather file their knuckles with a cheese grater than eat Metamucil. Instead, what works well for many cats is mixing one tablespoon of Libby's canned pumpkin with the food. You only need to do this once daily. It works because the amount of fiber is just about right for many cats. Other brands of canned pumpkin don't work. If none of this prevents constipation, better appeal to the court of last resort—your veterinarian. In some cases, special high-fiber diets work while other cats need in-depth diagnostic work like endoscopic biopsies. Be sure you take a constipated cat seriously—he could die.

Just a couple more points. *Never* use a Fleet or other type of phosphate enema on a cat. Because these can upset the electrolyte balance in cats, they can actually kill a cat. (They are OK for big dogs and humans.) Oh, and don't stand directly behind Scratchy while you give him the enema. You could learn a whole new meaning of graffiti art.

Long term: The truth is that many older cats will continue to have worsening problems with constipation. A surgery called a subtotal colectomy can permanently eliminate the problem. While there is some infection risk postoperatively, the great majority of these old-timers walk away from all that straining and never look back. If your cat has had more than a few bouts of serious constipation, talk to your veterinarian about the procedure. If he or she is not qualified to perform the operation, ask for a specialist referral.

Hookworms

A nasty parasite, they can also infect humans.

QUESTION:

What causes hookworms and what are the symptoms? Can my kitten be reinfested with them? (She is strictly an indoor cat.)

Dr. Nichol:

Hookworms are passed between cats and dogs by microscopic eggs and through the skin. Once inside, they bite into the wall of the intestine and suck blood. They cause weight loss, diarrhea, and anemia. If you fail to dump out your cat's litter pan after every use, your girl can become reinfected as you give her the medication to eliminate those worms. The good news is that your veterinarian can make short work of them.

Human infection: More folks are getting roundworms and hookworms from their pets. These parasites are the greatest risk to first-trimester unborn children, diabetics, the elderly, cancer patients, and those with HIV. To prevent risk to humans, every pet should have an annual stool exam.

Intestinal Parasites Can Put Your Cat at Risk—and You, Too

Have a stool check done for the kitty's health. Have a new kitten wormed for yours.

Question:

We got a new cat last week and took him to the vet for his first shots. After the doctor gave him the shot, he said that we need to bring in a stool sample to check Teka for worms. He also said Teka needs to be wormed anyway even if they don't find worms in his stool. Why not just worm the darn cat in the first place and forget the stool sample?

Dr. Nichol:

That piece of advice is really more about you and your family than about Teka. First, though, let's talk about Teka and his health.

There are about a half dozen different internal parasites that can infect pet cats in the United States. Some parasites are more dangerous than others, but any of them can cause weight loss, diarrhea, poor haircoat, and sometimes death. For the most part, each parasite requires a different medication to safely eliminate it from the cat's body. A fresh stool sample is important because it is examined under the microscope for parasite eggs. Since the eggs have a distinctive appearance, we can identify the type of parasite when we find eggs in the stool. Then we send home the right medication, get rid of the little creeps, and we all live happily ever after.

So, if it's that easy, why do we also give a wormer? That's the part that's for you. (No, *you* don't take the wormer.) It turns out that two of these parasites, roundworms and hookworms, are transmissible to people. An otherwise healthy adult would have little problem, but babies can suffer damage to their livers, brains, or eyes. But while stool exams are important, no lab test is 100-percent accurate. In fact, it is not rare for a pet with a belly full of worms to have a day when no worms lay eggs, thus showing us no evidence of the worms in the stool.

All of that being true, the experts in infectious disease have issued this advice. For the health of the pet, check a stool sample and treat for any parasites found. For the health of the family, make sure there is no risk of roundworm or hookworm infection by using a wormer that is effective against both.

Fortunately, we have one. It's cheap, totally effective, and even tastes good. (No, I haven't tried it—but I don't get any complaints either.) It does need to be repeated in three weeks, but so does Teka's vaccination. Its name is Strongid. Ask for it.

JOINTS AND BONES

Loss of Use of Rear Legs

Severe heart disease in cats can send blood clots to the arteries of the rear legs. A problem of sudden onset, it is painful. Have a full diagnostic workup done ASAP.

QUESTION:

My cat Button has twice lost use of her hind legs. My vet had suspected something parasitic going on, inflaming the disk space, and Button has now tested positive for heartworm exposure. She was not tested for this during last year's episode, as it is uncommon in this area. My vet says there are no approved methods of treating heartworm, and this is a very uncommon attack. I figure someone somewhere is working on this, and an unapproved treatment is better than none when death is the alternative. Button is only 3.

DR. NICHOL:

This is upsetting. There is no "approved" treatment for heartworms in cats but there are effective ways of managing most cases. My greater concern for Button is that her symptoms are not suggestive of heartworm disease because she does not have the typical signs of coughing, vomiting, and shortness of breath. Instead, her history is more consistent with a heart disease called cardiomyopathy. This can cause blood clots to the rear legs that may improve over time, only to repeat later. Cats with cardiomyopathy often drag their rear legs and cry out in pain. It's a terrible disease, but it's manageable in many cases.

The heartworm-positive test means that Button was exposed. To know more about this possibility as well as cardiomyopathy, have her chest X-rayed. In addition, a special ultrasound examination called an echocardiogram will determine not only which problem she has, but also help her doctor learn how best to treat it. I hope this helps.

Amputation
When is it the right thing to do?

QUESTION:

Our cat is 5 years old and we love her a lot. Yesterday she was runover by a car and the veterinarian said that her leg is so badly mangled that there is no way to fix it so she can walk normal again. The doctor told us that it's best to amputate Freckles's leg. We don't want to do this because we feel this is cruel for Freckles to be handicapped this way. Would it be kinder to have her put to sleep?

DR. NICHOL:

It is so upsetting to have a pet get so badly hurt. You want what is best for Freckles, but you want her pain to end. You can relax—the choice is much easier than you think.

Number one: With the exception of giant-breed dogs, almost all pets do just fine with three legs—especially cats. They simply shift some of their weight to each of the other legs. They develop their other muscles and learn to rebalance the load. But best of all, three-legged cats learn quickly to run, play, and climb trees.

Amputation sounds like an intensely stressful and painful operation for recovery. We give pain medication to our amputation cases, and they heal remarkably fast. They go home the day after surgery.

In terms of pluck and the resolve to play the hand they are dealt, pets—especially cats—can be an inspiration to us all. I say go for the amputation.

MOUTH PROBLEMS

Bad Teeth in Cats

Careful treatment and prevention at home. Better health and no mouth pain.

QUESTION:

I just had my 6-year-old male cat, Sam, to the vet for a checkup. Two of Sam's small, lower teeth have cavities, and they'll probably break off. What can I do to improve Sam's dental health? I don't think he'd let me brush his teeth.

DR. NICHOL:

I'm glad you're taking your cat's mouth seriously. My cat Raoul has a very nasty mouth, but in his case it's his rude comments more than anything else.

Start by having Sam's doctor clean his teeth and apply a fluoride treatment to harden the enamel. Teeth that are badly weakened or have exposed root canals may need extraction. On the other hand, they may be OK to be treated with tooth varnish or fillings. If he won't tolerate brushing, I would recommend feeding prescription diet t/d; your veterinarian has it. T/d is different because the teeth slice it when it's chewed, unlike regular dry food, which shatters when a cat bites it. It'll slow down tartar buildup. Lastly, keep in mind Sam's vulnerability and have him examined every six months. To me, you sound like a cat's best friend.

Age, Teeth, and Anesthetic Safety for Cats
Special lab profiles just for cats can uncover most concerns.

QUESTION:

At what age is it too old to allow my cat to have anesthesia? Our veterinarian is suggesting that we have Odie's teeth cleaned, but he's 14 now. I don't want to take a chance that Odie might not wake up.

DR. NICHOL:

I am glad to get this question. I hear it a lot from concerned pet owners at our hospital. The answer is that anesthetic safety has no direct relation to the number of birthdays. Instead, anesthetic safety is influenced by the following factors: physical condition; the type of anesthetic used; and the experience, training, and care of the personnel who administer the anesthetic.

Here are things you can do to make it safe for Odie: Insist that he have a thorough lab screening first. This should include a blood profile, blood count, and urinalysis as well as chest X-rays and ECG. Since many older cats have benign thyroid tumors, I advise a TT4 also. Assuming that Odie's lab work checks out fine, he should be a safe candidate for anesthesia as long as he is given a gas anesthetic accompanied by fluids IV.

Is it worth all that? As long as he is healthy and anesthesia is given safely, the answer is yes. If you neglect the need for dental cleaning, he'll pay much bigger later with infections, mouth pain, and maybe kidney trouble, too. Besides, I bet Odie doesn't think of 14 as "old."

Anesthetic Safety for Dental Cleaning

Oral health is too important to neglect. Lab profiles help make it safe.

QUESTION:

I have a 2-year-old cat, Livvy, who has never had her teeth cleaned. I have been told by my vet that this should be done annually, but I am terrified that Livvy will meet the same terrible fate as my friend's dog and my other friend's cat—they both died under anesthesia during dental cleaning. How necessary is it to give dental cleaning to a cat that eats dry food? Are there any checking questions I can ask of a vet to assure they are using the safest methods of anesthesiology?

DR. NICHOL:

You are right about anesthesia. If not done with great caution, it is not worth the risk. Livvy is mighty important to you. It's your job to keep her safe. So, what's the big deal about dental cleaning? Cats and dogs can get chronic gingivitis just like us. Tartar buildup will force Livvy's gums away from her tooth roots. She can get infections, loose teeth, cavities, and pain when she tries to eat. Imagine pretty Livvy with no teeth: No prom date. Tragic. Dry food is excellent, but tartar will still accumulate—just more slowly. But without anesthesia for the cleaning, your veterinarian will need anesthesia for facial surgery. Wide-awake kitties get upset when alien instruments go buzz in the mouth.

Livvy needs a thorough physical exam, a preanesthetic lab profile, safe gas anesthesia with oxygen, cardiac monitoring, and, most of all, a well-trained staff to watch her like a hawk while she slumbers through her dental cleaning. At our place, we do it right and the pets go home with a pretty smile.

New Pets in the Home; Cats Who Leave Home

━━━━━━━━━━━━━━━━━━━━━━━━━━━━━━━

Pets as Gifts

It may be a great idea. But the surprise of a real live long-term responsibility wears off fast. Talk about it first and be ready for the real investment of energy and expense.

QUESTION:

My fiancee has said that she might want a pet and I'm running out of time to get her a birthday present. I really love her and I want to see that look of joy on her face when she opens the wriggling box. What kind of pet do you think I should get her?

DR. NICHOL:

Boy, am I glad you asked this question. A major recent survey of pet owners showed that a full 70 percent of us regard our pets as children. Now that I have two human children, it's like having two more kids (or is that two more pets?). Either way, they touch your heart the same way. So, the answer to your question is, *do not make it a surprise*! Our emotional lives are complicated nowadays. If the object of your love gets a pet she is not ready to care for, she may keep the critter anyway because she won't want to hurt your feelings. But pets (except maybe goldfish) take time, commitment, and expense to manage properly.

So, here is what you do. Tell your heartthrob that you love her and that you want to share the joy and responsibility of raising a wild and crazy young dog or cat. (You can get her a gerbil or iguana, but cats and dogs are easier to bond to because they have emotions that are much closer to ours.)

Give her a chance to say "not now, later." If she decides to pass, don't feel rejected; instead take it as a sign of her maturity and ability to know when to commit and when the time is not right.

Lastly, I will tell you what you can do if you *really* want to share the commitment with your fiancee. Present your fiancee with a gift certificate for the vaccination series and the spaying or neutering. Now we're talking true love.

Roaming

Too many cats in a home may cause some the need to get more "space."

QUESTION:

Is this true that even if your female cat has been spayed, she still goes looking for a male? We have five cats and one of the females escapes. We live where coyotes come down off the mesa at night and hunt.

DR. NICHOL:

I understand what a frustration this must be. I couldn't bear the thought of losing my cat to a coyote. But to understand why this is happening, we must recognize the realities of who our cats really are. A spayed cat has no drive to mate. Your girl is no floozy. She comes from a good family, darn it. But there are two reasons for her to look for adventure away from home. First, cats are natural hunters. Second, they are not really community creatures but loners. While some tolerate sorority life, this one needs "her space."

To stay inside, she must have her natural needs met at home. Provide her a tall indoor scratching post with little carpeted hideouts and dangling funky toys to stalk, maim, and disembowel. It may be necessary for her to live with no more than one other cat. If she can live what is "normal" for her indoors, she shouldn't need to prowl the streets and have anyone question her moral character.

A Wild Cat Who Leaves Behind a Loving Home Life

How can a well-loved housecat leave home—for good?

QUESTION:

I had a long-haired Calico who was with me for eight years. We moved to a new house and two days later she dashed outside and I never saw her until ten months later. I tried to capture her; I did manage to grab her once and I ran back to my house, but she scratched me and I dropped her and she ran away. She had never been an outside cat before. She's not hungry, but she just doesn't want to be with me. She doesn't want to come home. Is there anything I can do or is this just her choice? I am at such a loss.

DR. NICHOL:

This must tear your heart out. We invest heavily in the love of our cats, but we can easily forget that there are some huge species differences with them. While your cat loved you in your home, you saw only one side of her personality. Because cats are not truly community creatures like most other mammals, they can easily revert to a solitary free-living existence. The apparent sudden change is what's hard. Behaviorists have learned that cats mature "socially" around 2.5 to 4 years of age. For your cat, this maturation amounted to a need to live her other life as a loner. The move to your new house provided the right stress and opportunity. Your girl's *call of the wild* was not your fault. Keep the memories in your heart alive, but let her go.

Choosing a Kitten? Be Careful When Considering a Manx

These cute pets with funky tails can develop nerve damage.

QUESTION:

I just love Manx cats—especially the ones with no tail at all. I had one as a child and I would like to get another. Any advice?

DR. NICHOL:

I share your love of cats. I cannot imagine living without at least one in my life—and you're right about Manx cats. They usually have great personalities. But there is an important problem to bear in mind and that is the reason for their interesting tails.

The tails of animals are really an extension of their vertebral columns (the backbone). It starts just behind the skull and is made up of a series of bones that are mostly block-shaped with a tunnel through the middle for the spinal cord (the bundle of nerves that supplies different parts of the body). In Manx cats, the vertebrae are the normal block shape from the skull to near the rump. Then their shapes can get bizarre and irregular. This is why some Manx tails are different lengths—often kinky in shape. For most Manx cats, the abnormally shaped vertebrae cause no problems. But in some it can mean trouble.

If the odd-shaped vertebrae develop in the lower back instead of just in the tail, the nerves that branch off the spinal cord can become pinched as the kitten grows. If the nerves that supply the bladder are pinched, the kitten loses the ability to control its urine flow. The result is not only a mess, but urine that stays bottled up inside the bladder. This leads to infection and often kidney failure.

There is no way, when choosing a Manx kitten, to know if it will end up this way. You will need to either accept this gamble or choose another breed of kitten—or best of all, a mix.

Death in a Family of Cats

Do cats in group mourn the loss of one of their own? This is how the survivors react.

QUESTION:

I know this might sound juvenile, but when you have three cats like I do, if one dies do the other cats know that one of them is gone? And if they do, how long does it usually take for them to adjust?

DR. NICHOL:

I don't think your question is juvenile at all. While our pets are part of our families, they also have their own social structure. Your cats know when changes occur, but they respond differently because they are a different species.

When cats behave like a person, it's because they recognize the leader and they allow that individual (you) to set the tone. But among your household cats, one of them is dominant. That cat has a heavy influence on the behavior of the others. If that cat leaves the group, you may see one of the others become much more assertive—maybe acting in new ways. It's also possible that with the loss of one kitty, there may be no changes.

How could that be if the hierarchy is upset? Most animal species, including humans, are highly social, meaning that removal of one member results in someone else filling the void. But cats are not really very socialized. They are loners by nature. In fact, a whole bunch of cats in one home may cause stress that can be manifested as physical disease. So the death of one of your cats may have no effect or it may bring out the "true" personality of one or more of the others. One thing that's unlikely is that the others would mourn the loss. Cats are not usually into weddings, birthdays, and funerals. There are never wakes, but the political deck does sometimes get reshuffled.

Introducing a New Dog to an Established Group of Cats

There is a good method to taking it slow and careful. A gentle dog should fit in well—eventually.

QUESTION:

Five days ago, I got a young dog. I already had three cats. I've let the cats run loose at night and kept the doggie in the bathroom. I let them all sniff under the door. I've taken the dog with me in the daytime and let the cats be able to go into her bathroom to check out her scent. I'm not comfortable letting her roam the house yet with the kitties. The cats are not hiding and are circling around staring at her when I bring her out on her leash in the house. She appears to want to play; they, of course, are disgusted . . . but also curious. I need to let the cats get nose-to-nose soon with her on the leash in case any fights break out. Do I interfere if they growl/spit? Just hold the leash so they don't chase and fight and talk soothingly? I talk to them all when they're in the same room. I also shut the cats away in the morning and let her roam the house where cat scent is. None are ever loose in the same room. The dog doesn't bark or growl other than a small woof each time. She seems to want to play and makes a "lunging" movement that appears playful. I expect this routine to last a few weeks at least. Then I'll let them all together only when I'm supervising with the dog off the leash. Am I doing this right?

DR. NICHOL:

I'm impressed. You have a fundamentally sound approach. Your basic understanding of the fear felt by your cats and the curiosity and playfulness of your young dog are on the mark. Here are a few points that will help the process along.

You have added two stresses to your group of cats. One is an additional creature in their already crowded household. The other is fear. The results of these new stresses may be physical disease. Or they may act it out with behavioral problems like urinating on your walls and furniture. They may also fail to accept this new family member—permanently. But let's work on it anyway; we still have a shot at a negotiated peace settlement.

Next, eliminate fear. Sit with your dog on a leash at one end of your house. Give her a rawhide chewy so she is not focused on the cats. Then let the cats out to explore the house with your dog visible. Repeat these sessions until everybody appears completely bored. Then, the final frontier. Get a 20-foot lightweight nylon cord at the hardware store. Sit with your dog with no toy and have the cord tied to her collar. Allow the cats to roam the house. Any aggression by your dog is corrected with a sharp jerk on the cord. As her behavior improves, allow her to leave your side but always with the nylon cord attached. Thus, the cats will learn not to run from her and she will not feel motivated to give chase. Lose the cord when you have confidence that this youngster fails to notice the existence of the cats.

Will it work? Only time will tell. Most dogs do well this way. Some are aggressive by nature and can't resist the hunt— and that can be deadly. Use your head. If your dog keeps failing the test, you better leave her outside.

"Found" Cats May Really Be Beloved Pets

Watch the paper, post signs, and have that cat scanned for a microchip.

Question:

I've had my cat Pancho since he was a baby 12 years ago. He's been through a lot with me. Now I have small children who love him, too. Even though he's a real independent cat, he likes to spend most of his time outside—he always comes home every day. But he disappeared three days ago. I'm real worried, and my kids are waking up at night crying for Pancho. He never goes near the road. I've talked to most of our neighbors, but nobody has seen him for three days. They usually see him every day. What can I do?

DR. NICHOL:

I know how worried you are. The same thing has happened to me and my cats. I know Pancho never intended to break your heart and sadden your children, but he is a cat. Needless to say, cats have minds of their own.

Statistics and experience show very clearly that outdoor cats are less likely to reach old age. The perils they face include altercations with dogs, automobiles, and other cats. All that catting around puts them at greater risk of infectious disease, too. So it makes a lot of sense to have only indoor cats—unless your cat will *not* stay in. Pancho sounds like a pretty street-smart cat. Surely he's learned to avoid dogs and cars by now. So, where is he? I will suggest an answer based on my years of experience of seeing "new" cats.

Here is how it goes. I walk into the exam room to see an adult cat brought in for its first visit to the doctor. The family is proud as punch of their new cat. I ask, "Where did you get this good-looking, well-cared-for healthy adult cat?" The answer comes back: "He just showed up" or "We found her on the road." Or the best one: "She followed the kids home from school." But the reality may be that this was not a stray cat at all, but someone else's beloved pet who also happens to be an adventurous opportunist.

Assuming for a moment that Pancho is enjoying the adulation of another family, it does not mean he loves you any less. It's just that most cats are perpetual teenagers. Thinking of it this way may cause you to resent folks who, in effect, steal pets. You're right. It is selfish. But the way the new family sees it is that they are saving the life of this homeless waif who would surely starve or be consumed by evil forces were it not for their generosity.

So here is my advice: Make some fliers for your neighbors. Include a picture. Point out that Pancho's children miss him. Also place a classified ad in the paper. Put his picture on milk cartons. Do whatever it takes to get the word out. As soon as he returns, be sure he has a tag with your name and phone number. And have a microchip implanted by your veterinarian (it takes a few seconds in the exam room) so that you can prove he is your cat.

To cat lovers who feel a duty to take in homeless pets: Consider the feelings of others. Any cat who seems remarkably tame for a stray may not really be a stray. If you find a cat, show compassion for the cat *and* the heartsick family who doesn't know how to find their pet. Print fliers, place an ad, and take the kitty to the Animal Humane folks to have him scanned for a microchip (this takes a second). For every pet who has gotten love, there is a person who has given love.

A Strong Case Against Multiple Cats in the Household

Having cats who get along well is a godsend. Gambling by adding more cats invites behavior problems in the group.

QUESTION:

We have two beautiful cats that are 2 years old. They are brother and sister indoor cats. The male is mellow, alert, and protective of both of us. He gets along very well with his sister. She does not like strangers. Quite the opposites, but both incredible cats! The question is: We would like to get another kitten, possibly two. What is your advice on this major decision? We do not want to disrupt the wonderful relationship we have with our animals, but would like to have more so they can have someone younger to be playful with and we would have younger ones when our original cats, unfortunately, pass away.

DR. NICHOL:

I wish more people would seek out this type of counsel. You know how we are. If we get pets who turn out badly, we are still in love with them. In other words, you can get stuck in a bad situation.

First and most important: Cats are *not* community animals. Unlike people, dogs, birds, and livestock, cats are naturally loners. So when we put house cats in groups, weird things can start to happen. Most often this amounts to urinations on beds or countertops but can also include fighting and reclusive behavior. Some multiple-cat households develop group infections. The bottom line is that community life for cats is stressful.

But wait. There's more. Your cats are established in your household. Newcomers may never be accepted. Howling and caterwauling may ensue and destroy your happy home. You could tear out your hair. You could lose your mind. Or it could work out fine—but that is a major gamble. Remember what I have said before: We treat our pets as children because they are so much like us. We share so many emotions and feelings with them. But there are some essential and striking differences. Don't try to fool Mother Nature. What you have now is working. If it ain't broke, don't fix it.

ODD NOISES AND INTERESTING HABITS

■ ■

Hyperactive, Yowling Older Cat

Hyperthyroidism can cause behavior changes. It can also be dangerous.

QUESTION:

My 15-year-old, spayed female, Siamese cat-mix walks around the house yowling constantly. She sounds just like a cat in heat. She does it day and night. She is otherwise completely normal: eating, drinking the same amount of water, using the cat box, the way her fur looks, etc. It is getting on our nerves so badly that my husband is threatening to have her put to sleep. Any ideas on what might be causing this?

DR. NICHOL:

I can appreciate why you need help. Without a solution to this yowling, you may want yourself put to sleep. There are a few plausible explanations for this behavior, but by far the most likely is hyperthyroidism. It's caused by benign tumors on the thyroid glands, which produce too much thyroid hormone. Aside from their bizarre behavior, these poor old cats often lose weight in the face of excessive appetites. Severe heart damage is also a common result of this disease.

The good news is that hyperthyroidism is quick and easy to diagnose with a blood test. Treatment is usually quite safe and effective. Now put down the gun and call your veterinarian.

Constantly Meowing Unspayed Cat
She'll be in heat most of her life until she's spayed.

QUESTION:

I have a cat that is not in heat that meows constantly. She is not deaf. This started about five months ago after her kittens were given away. The meows are deafening! It sounds as if she is in heat, but she is not (again, this has been going on for months). She does not seem to be in any pain as the meowing will subside for a few hours, then start up again. Any help would be appreciated for the cat's sake.

DR. NICHOL:

It's good to know that your cat is not deaf, although with her constant meowing I bet you wish you were sometimes. Let's fix this not only for the cat's sake, but for yours, too.

The reason your cat is meowing constantly is because she is in heat—*constantly*. Cats are usually in heat or pregnant at all times. The reason is that unlike the rest of us mammals, daylight is a major influence on their reproductive cycles. Between March and October, these girls are, well, waiting for gentlemen callers.

Won't she finally stop being so obnoxious and just "cycle" out of heat? Yes, but only when she is bred. Cats not only stay in heat during the warmer months; they stay that way until they find Mr. Right. (These are deeply meaningful relationships, but only for a few minutes.) At the time of breeding, they ovulate (release one egg for each kitten) and immediately go out of heat and shut up. Thus, almost every breeding with cats is a fertile one. They tend to have big families.

Your girl is talking about this all the time—not because she is in pain—but because she wants something done about her reproductive issues. What she is saying, in cat language, is "Have me spayed!" I know this. I'm a veterinarian and I talk to the animals.

A Family Cat Has Started to Wage War on the Dog

Look for changes in the dog's health that cause the cat's aggression.

QUESTION:

My cat and dog were the best of friends and then all of a sudden they are fighting like cats and dogs! My dog starts screaming this high-pitched bark/scream every time I walk out of the room and leave her alone with the cat. Her private area is swollen and looks sort of blackish in color around the opening with some leakage that smells and keeps matting up her fur. I've never owned a female dog before and I'm clueless.

DR. NICHOL:

Sounds like a pretty scary cat. The truth is that your kitty had grown accustomed to the normal smell of your dog and now look what's happened—he's living with an alien. The real issue is the health of your girl dog.

The list of causes for this discharge includes infections of the vagina, uterus, or bladder. Or she may simply be in heat. Occasionally a thick-coated dog like a Pomeranian can get an infection of the skin folds near the genitals. How do you figure out which of these maladies is besetting your dog and upsetting the delicate political balance in the animal kingdom you call home? As Dear Abby would say: Seek professional help. Take her to her veterinarian. She may need urine and blood tests as well as X-rays to learn the real cause. Treatment may range from antibiotics to an ovariohysterectomy to remove an infected uterus. If you wait, she could get very sick.

Now about that cat: He needs to learn to accept others as they are. Maybe he should get in touch with his female side. We'll work on him later.

Nighttime Activity

A yowling inside cat will keep you awake. There are ways to reset a cat's clock.

QUESTION:

About a month ago, our 6-year-old Birman male (neutered) started waking up in the middle of the night and wandering around the house yowling. I had his thyroid tested, and it was fine. I have also tried a program of keeping him awake during the day, but what an impossible task that is! Any suggestions?

DR. NICHOL:

You sound tired. I bet the reason you're having trouble keeping this boy awake is that you keep falling asleep.

The trouble with this party animal is that he's an active indoor cat who's trying to get you to pay more attention to him. He's sleeping soundly while you're gone during the day. Being a naturally nocturnal guy anyway, 2 A.M. seems perfect for some quality time together. If you chase him off when he yowls your name, well, you just rewarded his behavior by paying attention to him. If you feed him, he'll learn even faster to wake you even earlier. What he really needs is gainful employment. A few useful ideas include a large scratching post with enclosures, ramps, and tunnels. Add a couple of feathers-on-a-stick toys and a good time will be had by all. If he still craves attention during the wee hours, consider getting another cat as a playmate. If that doesn't feel right to you, an alternative would be to make him an indoor–outdoor cat. But if you go this way, be aware of the potential for disasters like auto injuries and fight wounds.

Last, if none of this works, you can give him the over-the-counter antihistamine chlorpheniramine (brand name Chlortrimeton). Two to four milligrams at bedtime with a late dinner and all could be peaceful—unless you yourself start yowling around the house and pestering your poor Birman cat.

Growling and Hissing at Neighbor Cats Through a Window

Gradual introduction to another cat will help overcome fear of strange cats.

QUESTION:

We have a kitten that's about 5 months old and stays indoors. She is the only pet we have. Her only problem is that whenever another cat comes to the sliding glass door, our cat hisses and yowls and throws herself at the window. This wouldn't be so bad, but it always seems to happen at night when I'm trying to sleep. What can I do to make her stop this?

DR. NICHOL:

With the help of folks like you who write in, we may be able to save a few lives. I'm serious. Behavior problems are the leading cause of death in pets because it is the biggest reason that pets are put up for adoption at animal shelters. Only 40 percent of dogs and 25 percent of cats in shelters find homes. The bottom line is that only one in three pets are in the same home two years after adoption. A great number die from euthanasia because their owners did not know how to live with them. If we can help fix a few behavior problems, we can make a dent in this tragedy. So keep the questions coming.

Understand first that the reason your cat does this is that she hasn't had enough exposure to other cats to feel comfortable when they visit. She feels threatened. Her aggressive behavior suggests that better social skills would help. Knowing this, one might assume that the more visits she gets from other cats, the more relaxed she will be. The opposite is true. So, handle this problem now and avoid worse trouble later.

To help your cat learn to play nice with her friends, we can use a behavior-modification technique called "flooding." Don't get her a boat. Instead, it means that we can introduce other cats to her gradually and nonthreateningly. The ultimate goal is for her to learn that she can be a cool kitty around other felines and not jar you from your sleep. The easiest way to do this will be to adopt a second cat (preferably a congenial kitten).

Start by keeping the new kitten in a separate room for a couple of weeks to allow him (or her) to adapt to your home. At the beginning, do not allow the two cats to see each other. When you are ready to start, give your cat her regular feeding, then sit at the other end of the room while gently holding the kitten. Your cat is sure to notice the other guy, but will continue eating. When your cat is just finishing her meal, sneak the kitten back into his private room and you are done with lesson number one. Easy, right? For your next trick, you will do the same thing, but you will sit or stand with the kitten a little closer while the grumpy one eats. You will do this at least a few times each day. Each time try to move a little closer. If the big girl starts to growl or hiss, you have moved the process along a little too fast; so you will need to back away a little. With me so far?

Things will go OK until old Sour Puss acts put out and just walks away from her dish. And this is good because now you can start to have a little fun. You will just whip out your feathers-on-a-stick toys (available at some veterinary clinics and pet supply stores) and start to entertain your cats by having them jump around and act goofy with their individual toys as you wave them one in each hand. This part of the process will take several sessions also because cats are, of course, resistant to change. Be sure to start out with the toys at the ends of your outstretched arms. As they begin to learn to play close to one another, you can move the toys closer together. Eventually, they may learn to share the same toy, fall in love, get married, have kittens of their own, contribute regularly to a 401(k) plan, and live happily ever after. Go ahead, admit it, you're getting a little teary-eyed, too.

What about other suggestions? Oh, they're much too easy. You could close the blinds so your cat can't see her visitors or put a Scat Mat in front of the window to discourage her from going near it. Things that don't work include spraying Cat-B-Gone or other repellents near the outside of the door. You could also develop your own neurotic habits, but you might end up at Animal Control yourself.

An Outdoor Cat Who Moves Inside a Small Apartment

Yowling, clawing, pacing, and generalized anxiety are common after a move to confined quarters. A snug den, fun indoor activities, and anti-anxiety medication should make the difference.

QUESTION:

My coworker recently moved to a small apartment where she has to keep her 5-year-old cat indoors. He used to be indoor–outdoor and is not happy. At night he wakes her with yowling, furniture-clawing, pacing, etc. She's getting pretty worn out after two weeks. I suggested she confine him in his carrier for short periods during her sleeping time when he goes nuts. The apartment will seem large compared to the carrier when he's out the rest of the day. Also, he can't scratch furniture when she can't squirt him. I figure he'll grow out of his anxiety if she does this. I told her to just quietly put him in the cage—no yelling, hitting, etc.

Do you think this will work for my friend's cat? I hate to see her get rid of this guy because he's making her life hell!

DR. NICHOL:

Such strong language. You want to know hell, try answering tough questions like yours. And one more thing: Is this really about your friend's cat? Is this really your cat? Or maybe he's not a cat at all. Getting rid of a guy who's making your life hell. . . . Is this about your boyfriend? See my picture? Do I look like Dear Abby?

OK, let's assume this is about your friend's cat. This little fellow has just gone through a life-changing experience. He has moved to a new home with no outside. That's tough for cats. These guys don't like change. His yowling, pacing, and furniture clawing simply means he's scared and anxious. There are three things that will help him adjust. (If we're talking about your boyfriend, add a lobotomy to the list.)

For starters, remember that cats are instinctively den animals. They naturally find comfort and security in a snug enclosure. Using a carrier (not too small, please) or a heavy plastic airline crate may give this boy the security he needs. She can make it comfy with a nice thick pad, some food, water, and a few kitty toys. Will this be enough by itself? Maybe. For most cats it will help; a few may get even more anxious. Give it a try.

The second ingredient for kitty adjustment is short-term use of an anti-anxiety medication called Buspar. Cats do very well with this because it's gentle. It has no tranquilizing affect. After a few weeks he should be fine and will not end up at the Betty Ford Center. The third factor in the success of this adventure is time. Patience will pay off.

Now, back to your boyfriend: Do you really squirt him when he gets on the furniture? Yelling and hitting before putting him in his cage? Maybe you just need a support group.

Inactive and Bored

Adding a second cat could be a disaster.

QUESTION:

I have a 10-year-old female indoor cat who is largely inactive and possibly bored. Do you think it would be a good idea to get her a cat companion? It's been just the two of us living together for over nine years. Would she welcome or resent another feline? She refuses to say!

DR. NICHOL:

This must be lonely-hearts day for pets. I don't want to sound like a broken record (nor a geezer for using that expression) but no, don't get another cat as a companion for your older cat. Only do it if you want one for yourself.

May I repeat my mantra? We are highly bonded to our pets because we share so many emotions—but they are different in some important ways, too. Cats, in particular, are not community creatures. Unlike people, they are meant to be solitary. If your girl cat were still a kid, she could learn to accept another kitty. But cats are conservative, and as they age, they just become even more stodgy. Be warned. If you get another cat, she'll hate his guts.

Licking People

Yucky. Is it normal? Why do some cats do this?

QUESTION:

Over the last couple of years my 14-year-old cat, Pita, has developed the habit of licking me on the hands, arms, and face as if bathing me. She also does this with cotton T-shirts I have worn. I have been wondering if there may be something lacking in her diet, or that she's getting senile.

DR. NICHOL:

I bet that rough tongue drives you crazy. Is the name Pita code for sandpaper mouth? Poor Pita may have been weaned too young and thus never matured out of the normal kitten behavior of mutual grooming and sucking. An easy experiment would be to give her a rawhide chew or a bone with a bit of meat still attached. If she relishes the experience and stops treating you like a Popsicle, your problem is solved. But I'm concerned that for Pita, there may be more to the story.

Behavior changes in older cats are often due to a problem called hyperthyroidism. The benign thyroid tumors that cause these excessive hormone levels are found in as many as 30 percent of cats over age 10. High thyroid levels can also cause serious heart disease and weight loss. A simple blood test will make the diagnosis. If Pita has hyperthyroidism, she's likely to do just fine with medication or surgical management.

What if Pita is physically normal? She may have a form of obsessive–compulsive disorder (OCD). One of several medications may be useful in turning off the abnormal chemical balance in her brain. Regardless of its cause, Pita isn't licking you to ingest missing nutrients. The human body is not a normal food group for cats.

A Dental Problem—or a Need to Roam?

A two-pronged analysis of a male cat's meowing.

QUESTION:

I have a 5-year-old neutered male cat. At a checkup at the doctor's office in October, they told me he has two teeth that should be removed. My concern is that he meows constantly in the evening and frequently in the early mornings. I live in a small studio apartment. When I take him out on the balcony, he stops meowing. He is driving me nuts. Can I make him stop this?

It's real easy to see how your kitty's complaining could make you crazy. Maybe you need family therapy. Just kidding. I have two recommendations.

First: Those teeth. I applaud you for getting him examined recently. Most pet owners recognize the value of annual vaccinations, but few understand that frequent checkups are even more important. Our pets age much faster than we do. By watching carefully, we can diagnose problems sooner and keep our pets healthier and living longer. If your boy has infections and tooth pain, he has plenty of reason for his misery. Start by having that dental procedure done for him. Relieving his pain could make all the difference in his grousing.

If he is still a chatterbox after his smile is fixed, he may simply need broader horizons. While some cats are content with life inside a small home, others require outside time. Cats are normally more active at night, but as we approach springtime, the increasing amount of daylight is another factor that could make a guy more active and want to be a part of that big world out there. For safety, add chicken wire to the balcony rail so he can't jump off. Plan his outside time each evening so that he can rely on his social hour. Mix him a drink and, hey, have one yourself, too, and join him on the balcony.

Cats Who Cover Their Food
Feline instincts influence protection of food resources.

QUESTION:

How can I get my cat to stop dragging rugs to cover the cat food dish? Is he hiding it from the other two cats to eat later?

DR. NICHOL:

Yes. Cats are loaded with instincts from their wild heritage. How could this be, you ask, given that they are the oldest domesticated pet? We don't know. Despite thousands of years of living with humans, cats seem unchanged from historical reports of the ancient Egyptians. They don't really live with us anyway. We live with them.

Anxious Cat Prowls the House at Night— "Meeping" Keeps Family Awake Causing "Insanity"

A recent move to a new home upsets the routine for this frightened cat. Time and modern medicine will ease the transition.

QUESTION:

We have a neurotic cat. Turtle has always been a touch compulsive and she's very meek. Always the low cat on the totem pole. We have a total of three. The latest problem: We just moved into a new house, and she's driving us insane. The first few hours, she explored and seemed OK, and then she started hiding in crevices and wouldn't come out for hours. Every morning now, for four mornings, she has woken up at 4:30 and wandered through the house "meeping," as we call it. Constantly crying out with short meows. Nothing we do comforts her. Is there anything we can do to calm her down (not only to make her feel better, but so that we can sleep until it's actually time to get up)?

DR. NICHOL:

I have known other meepers. While none of my behavior references list anything under "meep" or "meeping," this is a not-uncommon problem. What you have, of course, is a very anxious cat. Considering the conservative nature of most cats, it's never a surprise to hear about those who have difficulty with change.

In addition to having a hard time with an event such as moving to a new home, Turtle is easily frightened. This fear and anxiety are really just a function of her personality. Many cats are like that from birth and there is nothing you can do to make it better—except what you would do for anyone going through a difficult change. Be gentle and supportive—and give drugs.

Did I say drugs? If you want to improve everyone's quality of life in the short term, it's your only hope. You can just give Turtle's anxious meeping plenty of time, but you're getting sleepy. In time Turtle will finally adjust, but who knows how long it will take? In the interim, I suggest Buspar. This is an anti-anxiety drug that works well in most cats. The usual dose is one 5-milligram tablet every 12 hours. Ask Turtle's doctor for a prescription. It should start to help in one to two weeks, maybe sooner. While it won't cure Turtle's anxiety, it will diminish it until she adjusts to this big change in her life. This will also help you folks sleep better. Don't you dare take it yourself.

Lastly, here is what will *not* work: Tranquilizers. While the most commonly used and safest tranquilizer in cats is acepromazine, it won't help Turtle. Using it will cause her to stagger through the house while she slurs her meeping. This will only serve to embarrass her in front of the other cats.

Cats Who Hunt Compulsively

Predators by nature, cats can sadden their loving owners with the corpses they deliver to the door. An Ultrasonic Mouser can keep the mice at bay and prevent their demise at the paws of a pet cat.

QUESTION:

Miss Kitty is really a mister, but since I wanted a loving, cuddly cat, I named her Miss Kitty. She adopted us about 5 years ago, and I would guess her age to be 5 to 7 years. She is a nocturnal creature during the warm weather, and is constantly bringing home "presents" of birds, mice, rabbits, etc. Is there any way, short of confining her, to make her stop the hunting?

DR. NICHOL:

Perception is reality, isn't it? To you, Miss Kitty is loving and cuddly. The birds, mice, and rabbits would describe her differently. The bottom line, of course, is that Miss Kitty is a normal cat. It bears repeating that we bond to our pets because of the common emotional ground we share. They have feelings and needs just like we do. We are so bonded, in fact, that we can forget that cats are very different in some ways. Even though you give Miss Kitty an abundance of good food, she still feels compelled to act out her predatory instincts. All the same, it always hurts my feelings when I see a wild creature injured or killed by a pet cat. So, here is an alternative besides a bell on the collar or just keeping her inside. I was made aware of it by one of my readers from Santa Fe. "Another device is my Haverhill mouser (1-800-797-7367). I do not sell these things, but I was plagued (pardon the pun) with mice in the garage. I did not want to kill the mice, so I bought a Have a Heart trap. I was catching a mouse each night and could not find how they were getting in. I even painted a few on their bottoms so I could verify that they were not coming back. I installed the Haverhill ultrasound mouser and during over a month of operation I have caught only a single mouse so I am convinced that this thing works."

So there you go. There is no end to what a true animal lover will do. Just don't get caught painting the rear ends of field mice as you may get busted for some crime against nature. But you can tell me—your life with mice will be our little secret.

Plant Eating

There is no way to stop plant eating. Give the gift that keeps on giving: a Catnip Garden.

QUESTION:

We have an 8-year-old purebred Manx who seems to really love to eat plants. It was always a problem for the geraniums in his grandma's house when he lived there (she's happy to actually have plants now, since he would eat them all), and now he goes completely crazy when my husband brings me flowers. It seems he loves the baby's breath and the ferns that accompany the roses. We've heard that there are plants that are actually okay for kitties to chew on. Could you recommend some that we could purchase and leave on the floor for him to nibble on? Or is there a change we should make in his diet to satisfy his craving?

DR. NICHOL:

Aren't cats sneaky? Here your husband, new-age sensitive guy that he is, brings you flowers and your cat goes crazy. Maybe they were never your flowers in the first place.

Let's start with diet. It's not his diet. Cats aren't really vegetarians. There is nothing about house plants that he needs. But I do believe your cat is bored. To help him lead a more balanced life, I recommend a hobby. Go to your local pet supply store and purchase a Catnip Garden for $1.99. You grow the stuff yourself and your kitty can enjoy his own botanical delights, leaving you and your husband to share the ferns and baby's breath. Catnip is perfectly safe. In addition, you can provide other healthy activities such as a ceiling-height cat tree with carpeted little houses. Cats love to run up and down and play hide and seek in the enclosures.

Of course, there are alternatives to providing your cat with his own garden. In other words, something to bring out his gentler side—like rodent mauling. (Believe it or not a new kitten owner recently announced, with great pride, that she had purchased a pet for her new baby to keep him occupied. You'll never guess—a hamster. I suggested that the hamster may not fare well, but I was assured that the kitten is quite gentle and that the hamster is oblivious. Oh, brother.)

Now, back to boredom: If you leave out the catnip all the time, your cat will get bored with it. Instead, bring it out whenever you expect your husband to show up with a bouquet. This way your cat can go completely crazy over his catnip (something all cats do), leaving you to enjoy your roses in peace.

Poisoning

■ ■

Inducing Vomiting

Ipecac is best and safest.

QUESTION:

I have read that I should make my pet vomit if she swallows poison. I'll bet there's not one layman in 500,000 who knows how to make a cat vomit. Please tell me how to do that.

DR. NICHOL:

There are several effective methods including oral salt or hydrogen peroxide. Each of these can be dangerous. The safest is Syrup of Ipecac, which is available in little tiny bottles at any pharmacy. This is an over-the-counter product. The dose is one teaspoonful per 5 to 10 pounds of body weight—but no cat should get more than three teaspoonfuls. If your cat fails to vomit in 20 minutes, repeat the dose. Any pet owner or parent of small children would be well advised to keep a few bottles on hand in case of accidental poisoning.

Tylenol Poisoning

Cats can die quickly from just one dose. Emergency medical attention is needed fast.

QUESTION:

My 2-year-old cat, Bebe, swallowed an Extra-strength Tylenol a couple days ago. I took him to a vet and he's currently undergoing treatment. The test results show no signs of kidney damage, but they say his liver has been damaged. Can he continue to live an otherwise normal life? Would it mean constant medication? If you could shed some light as to what's to come, I'd really appreciate it.

DR. NICHOL:

You did the right thing in getting your cat to the doctor fast. It turns out that over-the-counter drugs are the fourth leading cause of poisoning in pets, with Tylenol (generic name: acetaminophen) topping the list. It's potentially deadly in cats and can be nearly as bad for dogs. The problem is that we get so connected with the feelings we share with our pets, we forget that there are some major physical differences.

As safe and useful as acetaminophen is for people, it is a horrible poison for cats. Even part of a tablet can kill. As soon as acetaminophen is absorbed into the bloodstream of a cat, it damages the red blood cells. About one to four hours later, a poisoned cat will become physically depressed and breathe rapidly. This is usually followed by vomiting, drooling, and brown-purple gums. Often their faces and paws will swell. But that's only the beginning. Cats can't eliminate acetaminophen from their bodies the way we can. Instead, they release a toxic substance that damages their livers, lungs, and kidneys.

This is really horrible—and treatment, while sometimes successful, can be prolonged and expensive. The first priority is to rinse out the poisoned cat's stomach. A medication called acetylcysteine is given IV along with fluids and other supportive care. A few cats have full recoveries, but most need long-term treatment for liver fibrosis.

The future management of your cat will depend on the severity of his liver damage. A prescription diet plus daily medications and periodic lab tests could be necessary to keep him going. I wish the best for you and Bebe.

[**Note:** The above is the response I sent to this worried cat owner. But afterward I received an update saying that Bebe's health had turned for the worst and he passed away. By Saturday night, an X-ray showed that his liver had shrunk to one-third the normal size and X-ray images of his lungs were cloudy, probably due to fluid buildup. Though he was not expected to survive more than 36 hours, he fought on for six days. "I would appreciate it if you would use my question in your newspaper column," the owner wrote me. "I had no idea one little Tylenol tablet could be so harmful to a cat, and I'm sure a lot of pet owners out there don't know either."

I told this man that I would do my part to alert caring cat owners. I ask everyone who reads this to spread the word.]

Antifreeze Poisoning: A Risk for Outdoor Cats

Malicious or accidental disasters: Cats who roam can break your heart. An Invisible Fence can keep them safe in your yard.

QUESTION:

Our cat Samson has been a healthy outside cat for a long time. Suddenly, about a week ago, he stopped eating and started to throw up. Since then he has begun to eat a little bit but he is drinking a lot more water than he ever has. Thinking back, the only thing different that happened was that he seemed to get sick right after we changed the antifreeze in the car. Can you tell us what's wrong with Samson?

DR. NICHOL:

It sounds very much like Samson was poisoned by the antifreeze. Even though he has begun to eat again, he is still very sick. When you take him to his doctor, blood and urine tests will be done that are likely to confirm ethylene glycol toxicity (antifreeze poisoning). With this diagnosis, Samson will be treated for kidney failure. This will involve several days of hospitalization for IV fluids and medications to prevent nausea and vomiting. If treatment is started quickly, Samson should improve, but he will always have kidneys that are prone to failure. Lifelong medications and a special diet will help him live as long as possible.

This is a very serious and common problem. In the fall, many of us change the antifreeze in our cars. Even a small amount (two or three teaspoons for a cat; two or three tablespoons for a 50-pound dog) will kill. We see it a lot because of the sweet taste—these little guys will race for it and lap it up quickly. Within 20 to 30 minutes after being drunk, the ethylene glycol in the antifreeze forms crystals in the kidney tubules. Symptoms include trembling, vomiting, seizures, coma, and death. It is treatable, but because of the rapid action of this poison, we have to start fast—before symptoms appear, if possible.

Is it OK to just watch a pet who was seen drinking only a small amount—just to be sure that treatment is necessary? Unfortunately, this is not a good option. Even minute amounts of antifreeze will cause permanent kidney damage.

Bottom line: If you plan to change your own antifreeze, lock up your pets and *thoroughly* clean up any spills. Or better still, use Sierra-brand antifreeze. Sierra has propylene glycol instead of ethylene glycol. It is nontoxic, as well as harmless to our environment. Regular antifreeze is unsafe on both counts.

Beware of Mouse and Rat Poison

D-Con and other rodent bait stops normal blood clotting. Death can occur quickly.

QUESTION:

I'm worried about my cat and I hope you can help me. He's a cat who goes outside a lot, but sleeps in the house at night. Yesterday he started acting kind of sluggish and today he has a lot of blood in the litter pan. So I looked in his mouth today and his gums look real pale—almost white. I call him Mouser because he catches lots of mice. What can I do for him?

DR. NICHOL:

I share your concern for Mouser. I suspect that he may have been poisoned. He is in grave danger and he needs medical attention fast. The reason you need to move quickly is that he may be bleeding internally.

We know that Mouser catches a lot of mice. It is possible that you have a neighbor who uses a rodenticide (mouse and rat poison) to get rid of the mice on his property. These poisons kill rodents by damaging their normal blood-clotting mechanism. Every one of us (including critters) needs normal blood clotting because throughout our day we often bump ourselves without noticing it. Little blood vessels are damaged and we bleed internally very slightly. But because our blood clots normally, that little vessel stops leaking right away and we don't even get a bruise. But what happens when a mouse or cat or anyone can't clot normally? We just continue to leak blood—until we bleed to death.

Rodenticides are poisons that taste good to rats and mice—and to cats and dogs, too. You may have some of this stuff at home. D-Con is the most common brand. When the D-Con starts to act on the rodent's body, internal bleeding occurs and they get weak and easy for a cat like Mouser to catch and eat. In recent years this poison has been made far more potent. There is easily enough D-Con in the body of a dying mouse to kill a large dog. When a pet like Mouser eats a poisoned mouse, the poison is absorbed into the pet's body and begins to damage his blood-clotting mechanism, too. The result is a cat with internal bleeding. The tipoff in Mouser's case is the blood in the urine and the pale gums.

What can we do? First, we can check his blood. If he is severely anemic (low numbers of red blood cells), he will need a blood transfusion. Next, we will need to get his clotting factors functioning normally again. Fortunately, there is an antidote: vitamin K-1 injections (*not* vitamin K-3). Once he is stable, he can go home on an oral form of K-1 for three to six weeks. The tablets are expensive, but without them you will lose Mouser.

This problem is frightening. The morale of the story is: Don't use mouse and rat poison. Pets are too easily made accidental victims. If your cat is a mouser like Mouser, talk to your neighbors and ask them to avoid rodenticides. Offer to share your cat if you have to. Give your neighbors their own cat. Use a neutron bomb. Do anything. Just don't let anybody in your area use poison.

SAFETY TIPS

Garage Door Openers
That "safe" door might not be.

LETTER:

I received this input from grieving cat lover, Tanya Gross: "I sure wish I'd asked about the safety of garage door openers before my cat, Big Louie, was fatally crushed by my 'safe' garage door. My new opener had sensor lights, but they were set too high off the ground (at $8\frac{1}{2}$ to 10 inches). Louie limboed under the sensors as the door was moving downward. The back-up safety feature, auto reverse, was never adjusted, so the door came down with crushing force.

"The recommended setting for the sensor lights is 4 inches to protect pets. Folks who set sensors at bumper height could be inviting disaster for small children and pets. The auto reverse should be tested monthly using a board or a crushable cardboard box. For more information, you can call the Genie Company at 1-800-654-3643."

DR. NICHOL:

Tanya, thanks for sharing this essential protective tip. I can speak for every one of our readers in sharing the pain of your loss of Big Louie. By spreading the word you may be saving the life of another pet or even a toddler.

Cats and Clothes Dryers
The warm enclosure invites cats. Inadvertently starting the machine leads to a terrifying death.

LETTER:

This letter is to warn other cat lovers. My $2\frac{1}{2}$ -year-old cat, Katie, died in May 1996. She had always loved to lie on the clothes coming out of the dryer. I should have paid closer attention to her habit. One morning I was going to refluff the towels in the dryer. I shut the door and turned it on. I heard a thumping noise, but rationalized it in my mind as wet towels. Twenty minutes later I found my precious baby— she was gone.

I have two cats now and Daisy has gotten into the dryer several times, but I was there and got her out. Check everything—the oven, the dishwasher, the washer, even the recliner and hide-a-bed. Cats find the most secluded and comfortable places to sleep. I'd hate for anyone to go through what I've gone through.

DR. NICHOL:

You have endured a terrible loss. It's clear that you still feel the pain over the death of Katie. Know that her passing was not in vain. By making other cat lovers aware of the hazard of clothes dryers, you have prevented the loss of other beloved pets.

Fortunately some cats are discovered in the dryer in time. But the injuries can be tough to manage. Not only do they suffer from severe heat exhaustion, but multiple skin burns as well.

Fanbelt Injuries

Cats love a warm, cozy spot on cold winter nights. Horrible trauma occurs when the car is started.

QUESTION:

Our neighbor's cat got stuck in the fanbelt of his car last week. How common is that? How do I make sure that doesn't happen to my cat?

DR. NICHOL:

Great question. I'm delighted to hear you thinking about prevention. The truth is that automobile fans and fanbelts kill and maim many cats every fall and winter. It is tragic but preventable. It happens because it takes awhile for a car engine to completely cool down even on a cold night. Cats naturally love snug enclosures anyway. So if it's a warm and cozy spot, your kitty may find it downright inviting. Often a cat will spend a whole night snuggled up against an engine. Then, when you start the car the next morning, the cat is suddenly hit by the spinning blades of the fan or cut or burned by the friction of the fanbelt.

The injuries are frightening. These kitties sometimes don't survive. Those who do usually have wounds of the face and rear end that sometimes include broken bones. The best way to keep your cat safe is to either keep her indoors at night or scare her out from under the hood before turning the key. You can do this by thumping on the hood a couple of times or blowing the horn. When the weather gets warm again, you can stop worrying. Thanks for caring this much for your cat.

■ ■

Staggering, Rolling, and Yowling

Vestibular disease is actually harmless. Affected cats recover.

QUESTION:

Recently we had to bring our 10-year-old cat in for symptoms that later showed she had vestibular disease. Our veterinarian was unable to tell us very much about it, because there wasn't really that much information available. My family and I are just trying to understand better what's going on with our cat, and how long it lasts.

DR. NICHOL:

This is a really scary problem when it suddenly appears. But the good news is that it should start to improve on its own in just three days. Cats with idiopathic vestibular disease (impressive name) are usually normal in two to three weeks. Treatment is seldom necessary.

So, what is this disease? There are things we know about it and things we don't know. We know it's caused by an abnormal flow of fluid in the part of the inner ear that controls the sense of balance. Cats with vestibular disease get disoriented, roll on the floor, howl and yowl, and get frightened when picked up. If they could talk, they would tell us how scared they are. We don't know what causes it. Those cats who recover from it are unlikely to get it again. It does not appear to be contagious.

But knowing that your kitty will be fine still isn't enough. She needs to feel better. We like to manage them at home unless they are too disoriented to eat or drink on their own. In those few cases IV fluids, sedation, and feeding tubes may be necessary for a day or two. Otherwise, I prefer home care: a darkened, quiet room, and soothing music. Minimize the rap.

Seizures and Circling

Brain tumors in cats are usually treatable. Acting early can return an older kitty to her old self.

QUESTION:

I am really worried about my cat. She's been sleepy and inactive for awhile. Lately she's walking like in a circle. She acts blind. She even had a fit. Our vet has done tests and X-rays. The vet said she might have a brain tumor. She wants us to take her for a scan. It sounds horrible.

DR. NICHOL:

You are right to be concerned, but your kitty may actually do quite well. My first advice is that you follow the doctor's recommendation. Take her to the neurologist (a specialist in diseases of the nervous system) for a CT scan of her skull. They will be looking for evidence of a brain tumor called a meningioma. If they find a mass on the outer surface of her brain, they will recommend surgery.

Is this risky? Believe it or not, in trained hands, it is not. In fact, cats respond very well to this surgery and are usually much better within a few days. But time is of the essence. Your veterinarian has given you sound advice. Move ahead quickly to prevent further brain damage.

Skin Problems

Surgery Wound Care

Keep the incision clean for good healing.

QUESTION:

We adopted a kitten from a local animal shelter two days ago. She had to be spayed before we brought her home. Do we have to do anything to keep the incision site clean? Or put any kind of ointment on it?

DR. NICHOL:

Congratulations on your new baby! I admire you for sharing your home with this little orphan. You just may have saved her from euthanasia.

I advise gently dabbing the incision with a moist wash cloth twice daily until the stitches are removed—about ten days after the surgery. Do not use hydrogen peroxide as this tends to be damaging to the tissues. Ointment would seem like a good idea, but studies have shown that for normal skin, oily stuff actually slows healing.

Fly Larvae Under the Skin

Harmless larvae can mature beneath the skin, drop off, and then move on to their next life stage. Your cat as a mule.

QUESTION:

How do you get a wolf worm to come out of a cat's neck?

Dr. Nichol:

Wolf worms. I've been a student of parasitology for a long time and I can find no reference to this name. We do, however, see bott fly larvae imbedded under the skin of cats. These go by the scientific name of Cuterebra and they're actually pretty interesting. It's a parasite that's related to the stomach botts of horses and cattle.

The larva that's stuck in your cat's neck can also infect rabbits, squirrels, mice, and dogs. Quoting from a recent text: "The eggs are laid in rodent burrows. The larvae penetrate the skin and in about one month, develop into stout grubs two to three centimeters long and beset with large black spines. The female fly uses a slave to carry her eggs to a prospective host. She captures mosquitoes or stable flies and glues her eggs to their abdomens. The eggs ripen in one to two weeks and the larvae inside them stand ready to disembark when the slave fly alights upon the skin of a warm-blooded animal to feed." And you thought *your* life was weird. You could have been born a bott fly destined to spend your life searching for slaves upon which to glue your eggs. Far out.

What your cat has is a swelling of the skin with a small hole that, believe it or not, is used by this spiny larva for breathing. You can wait for it to get bigger and drop out on its own or you can have it removed by a minor surgical procedure—a local anesthetic and a quick prep. If I were your cat, I would chose the latter.

Fleas

Here is how to get rid of them and stay rid of them.

Question:

I have been treating my cats with Advantage. Now they have worms from ingesting a flea. I have a dog that apparently brings the fleas into the house. I have been treating the worms with a medication called Droncit. Is it safe for my cats to be treated with this medication often? The fleas seem to be returning.

DR. NICHOL:

You are struggling with some of the toughest, meanest, wiliest, most low-down, no-good varmints that a pet can ever have: fleas. On the other hand, the tapeworms the fleas carry are almost totally harmless. The Droncit that your veterinarian has prescribed is quite safe and effective against tapeworms. But your primary pest priority is those darn fleas.

As chemical warfare has improved, so has the ability of fleas to adapt. These cunning bugs can survive most over-the-counter insecticides. If you use a truly effective treatment like Advantage on your pets, the fleas will live off skin flakes and dander in your pets' bedding. If you attack on the bedding front, the fleas just migrate outside. Your only hope is to move on all fronts using the following: Frontline Plus on your pets' skin, (which now includes a "growth inhibitor" to eliminate fleas from your home) and Dursban yard spray. Give Program tablets monthly for long-term management. I like Program because it's inert in the body of our pets. But inside the flea larvae it inhibits formation of "chitin" which they need to cut their way out of their eggs. Without their chitin "teeth," the larvae stay inside their nasty little eggs and rot.

So your dog is the "Typhoid Mary" of the household? All that means is that your family fleas don't care what mammal they suck on: dogs, cats, humans—no problem. A blood meal is a blood meal. Have your veterinarian provide the full array of weaponry and get tough.

Cat Fight Wounds

Abscesses are common result of cat fights. Know how to treat them at home and when to see the veterinarian.

QUESTION:

My cat is a boy about 5 years old who gets into a lot of cat fights. He's been neutered but we have a lot of cats in our neighborhood, so I guess he's just going to keep coming home with these wounds. Here's my question: Should I be using hydrogen peroxide to clean out these wounds? It sure seems to fizz up and make the pus go away.

DR. NICHOL:

Good question. The answer is no. Do not use hydrogen peroxide. Here is why.

This stuff works because it breaks down degenerate organic matter by oxidation, hence the foaming—in other words, those are oxygen bubbles. But while it's doing that, it's also harsh on the normal tissue in the wound. This delays healing and causes pain. But the worse part is the risk of embolism. While it is not common, open bleeding vessels can take in oxygen from those bubbles. If those bubbles reach the brain or heart, you could lose your kitty. So lose the hydrogen peroxide.

Clean those wounds, but use soap and water. Gently soak off the scabs at least three times daily. Do *not* let the wound heal on the skin surface for at least three days so that any discharges on the inside of the wound can escape. What you are preventing is trapped bacteria inside a wound. This would result in an abscess that can lead to severe tissue death.

But while it's important to apply first-aid, also know that if the wound swells, drains, or smells badly, you should see your veterinarian. It's OK to play doctor with your cat. Just don't get carried away.

Losing Fur in Clumps

With short but normal hair beneath the clumps, a cat may just be overdue for his spring shed.

QUESTION:

When I moved [to New Mexico] last summer from Massachusetts, I brought with me my 12-year-old female domestic long-hair cat. Recently, I have noticed that her fur is coming out in handfuls. I looked closer and found that I could easily "pinch" out a gob of hair by gently pulling on the base of the hair. (I didn't do this much though.) She does not, however, have any bald spots, but I did find a small spot that looked as though a different textured and darker colored hair has grown in. Could this be disease, age, or is she adjusting to the new drier, warmer climate? (Also, hairball production has been greatly reduced lately.) What should I do for Reggie?

DR. NICHOL:

Reggie's situation is common and we get this question often. But I'm still glad you asked. Some people might have just started using Rogaine.

I will start my answer with a qualifier: Without an up close and personal physical exam, it won't be possible to be certain of my diagnosis. Having said that, the diagnosis is: normal. Here's how I know. Reggie is a girl who has come from a different climate—that's one factor. In addition, she is a long-haired cat who, through the past fall and winter, may not have fully shed her summer coat. Shed her *summer* coat? Yes, ma'am.

Many folks don't realize it but our pets shed their coats twice yearly; that is, they shed a winter coat each spring and a summer coat each fall. With long coats like Reggie's, it's easy for the hair that is shed in the fall to get tangled and matted in the new undercoat of the winter. Now that the daylight is getting longer with the approaching spring, Mother Nature is saying, "OK, let's get rid of that old winter coat." So the whole works comes loose at once. And since most of that old matted dead hair has long ago been released from the skin, it pulls away from her new crop of spring hair with ease. That's why there are no bald spots underneath. That's also why she doesn't need Rogaine.

As far as reduced hairball production is concerned, I'm glad. To help Reggie along with this, get a "slicker brush" from your pet supply store or veterinarian's office. This is a brush with rows of claw-shaped wire bristles mounted in rubber. You can bear down pretty hard on Reggie's coat and get a whole bunch of dead hair loose. She'll enjoy it. But understand first that without her dread locks, she'll need to join a different clique in school.

Constant Irritation of the Tail and Amputation

A severely self-destructive problem that can drive a cat crazy.

QUESTION:

Our cat's tail was oozing bloody fluid and the surgeon amputated, leaving about a 2-inch stub of a tail. She is perfectly adjusted to it now. While we never had the tail specimen analyzed, we do have it at home in formaldehyde.

DR. NICHOL:

I, too, have seen cats who have suddenly begun to lick and chew their tails to the point of severe damage. While cleaning and bandaging the wound can be helpful, some of these cats will continue to go after their tails with a vengeance. In some cases, only amputation of the tail eliminates the problem.

The severe pain and irritation that drives some cats to do this has always been confined to the tail. The destruction of the tail is an interesting disease. I have made a search of the neurology literature and I have failed to find it described as a specific diagnosis. Yet, I know other veterinarians who have encountered this. While none of us wants to remove part of a kitty's body, the damage and infection that result from this problem can get so bad that tail amputation becomes a welcome alternative. In my experience every cat whose tail was amputated has gone on to do just fine.

So, in the case of your kitty, we could have a pathologist examine the tail specimen and provide some answers. On the other hand, your cat may feel an attachment to her tail—even though she has lost her tail over this problem.

Symptoms of Sickness

When to Go to the Veterinarian
How sick is that kitty anyway?

Question:

My cat has had all of his shots plus a recent tapeworm shot. He has been lethargic and drool has been pouring from his mouth. He has not lost his appetite and is currently drinking more water than usual. Should I take him to the vet $$$?

Dr. Nichol:

I think I understand your problem. Your kitty is eating, but not feeling well. Clearly his drooling and excessive drinking are not normal. But is he really sick enough to justify the expense ($$$) of a visit to the veterinarian? Or, put differently, will he get better on his own or will he just get sicker if he doesn't see a doctor?

Cats are special to those of us who love them and share our homes with them. They're different from dogs and people in that they complain less; maybe that's part of their appeal. It's also what makes it hard to recognize when they are in trouble. Typically a cat who is sick just lies low and tries to be inconspicuous. There's a good reason for it considering the instinct of self preservation. Only the strong survive in the wild. A kitty who advertises his illness by grousing about it is more than a nuisance—he's somebody's lunch. Your cat may be sicker than you think.

We have special challenges in veterinary medicine because our patients can't tell us what's wrong. We rely heavily on the observations of the pet's family. Cats make it harder still in that they tend to hide their disabilities by being less active. So, here are some important questions that will help you decide if your boy is really sick. Does he go outside? Does he chew house plants? Any vomiting or diarrhea? Is he passing more urine than normal? You said that he has had his vaccinations and an injection for tapeworms. Did his symptoms start the same day?

Now that I've added more uncertainty, I'll try to provide a few answers. If this boy goes outside, I would be concerned about antifreeze poisoning. This sweet-tasting toxin can quickly damage kidneys, causing drooling and increased thirst. On the other hand, if he's just sucking on the bitter leaves of indoor plants, I would shake my finger at him and explain that he has just reaped the consequences of his bad behavior. How about other symptoms? If he has vomiting and/or diarrhea, he may have other serious trouble. Important concerns here would have to include intestinal disease, organ failure, and maybe diabetes. Lastly, if he got his injections the same day, he may just have a stress reaction. But whatever you do, do not give him an aspirin and call the doctor in the morning. Aspirin, ibuprofen, and especially Tylenol will make for a much sicker kitty.

So, what about the expense? I wish money didn't have to be a factor, but let's face it—it is for a lot of folks. You love this guy and want him to have the very best, but if he'll get better anyway . . . Here's what you can do. Call your veterinarian's office and ask for a little telephone advice. Provide all the information you can. If they say that they better take a look, do as they suggest. No way do they want your kitty to take the wait-and-see approach if they think he'll be at risk. And if you take him to the doctor, remember that you're the boss. The veterinarian has two jobs. First, to diagnose and make treatment recommendations. Second, to do as you ask. I say you are smart to be concerned. Just don't gamble with the health of your cat.

Wet Noses

Wet nose, dry nose—no big deal.

QUESTION:

Should my cat have a wet nose? In the mornings, his nose is wet. He did have an upper respiratory infection when I got him at the shelter.

DR. NICHOL:

Assuming the infection has resolved, your cat can have a wet nose because of excessive tearing. Are you making your cat upset? Does he read romance novels in bed? Some of my best friends have wet noses and I'm not complaining.

Butt Dragging

Anal gland disease and the itchy rear end.

QUESTION:

My indoor pet Siamese cat has recently begun dragging her butt across the floor. She has never been outdoors, and I really am clueless as to the cause of the problem. What could be causing this?

DR. NICHOL:

Mmmmm. Sounds like me after a tough week at the animal hospital. Maybe she just needs a vacation. Oh, I forgot—cats are always on vacation.

OK, let's talk about physical reasons for this rather socially unacceptable behavior. For starters, I'll tell you what is *not* going on: She does not have worms. The type of worm associated with anal irritation is pinworms. There are two species:

one is a parasite of horses; the other, a cause of unending embarrassment for the parents of elementary school children. I will avoid that subject because the Nichol boys are elementary school children who, for the record, are not behaving like your cat.

The reason for your kitty's itchy rear end is almost certainly her anal glands. Now, this is not a pleasant subject so you may want to finish your lunch before you read on. These nasty little structures are similar to the scent glands of the skunk. For cats and dogs, they are nothing more than a pain in the . . . you know what I mean. There is one anal gland on either side of the anus. They secrete a foul-smelling fluid that normally flows out by itself as the pet goes about its daily life. But your unlucky cat has anal glands that have become full and may even be infected. If we don't empty them for her, she may develop a drainage of pus as her body tries to rid itself of this mess.

Your job is to take your kitty to her doctor soon to have those glands emptied. If they are infected, an ointment will be infused and antibiotics will be dispensed. Then, life will go on and, hopefully, she'll never look back.

Diabetes

Learn about this difficult disease and how best to control it.

QUESTION:

My 13-year-old cat has recently been diagnosed with diabetes. My doctor has me injecting him twice a day with insulin before his meals. I feed him one-quarter small can of w/d in the morning and one-quarter can at night with some crunchy food on the side. I have talked with another cat owner who only gives her cat one shot a day and less food at night. Do you recommend one method over the other? I would much rather only have to give him one shot a day. He would prefer this, too, I'm sure!

DR. NICHOL:

I know exactly what you mean. As far as I'm concerned, less is more when it comes to injections. But diabetes mellitus in cats is a creature unto itself. I can tell that your veterinarian is savvy about this awful disease. While once-daily insulin injections are easier for everyone, every 12-hour administration may be best for your cat.

Those of us lucky enough to have a normally functioning pancreas never think about insulin. But we all need it to survive. Here's how it works: The pancreas in cats is a few inches long and sits next to the small intestine near the stomach. When we aren't eating, it rests. But as soon as food arrives in the stomach, the pancreas goes right to work and secretes the hormone insulin. As the sugar from the digesting food absorbs into the blood, the insulin is already there to carry that sugar into the body's cells. But a diabetic is in trouble. The diabetic's pancreas has little or no ability to make insulin. Sugar builds up in the bloodstream, but has no way of getting into the cells. The cells cry out to the brain "Hey, we're starving out here!" So the brain turns on the hunger. Meanwhile, there's a whole lot of sugar in the blood. This causes the kidneys to let go of a lot of water in the urine. So the diabetic needs to eat, drink, and urinate more.

We give insulin by injection. If we give it just once a day, there has to be food in the stomach when the insulin reaches its peak blood level, usually several hours after being injected. If the insulin and the blood sugar are at their highest levels at the same time, things work fine. But the rest of the day your cat may eat food that does nothing but cause trouble. If you give insulin twice daily, you have a cat who feels better and whose body functions better much more of the time.

I know it's hard. But the needle on the insulin syringe is really tiny. Pinch the skin a few times before injecting to make it a little bit numb. Then feed your kitty as soon as you're done with the injection. Most cats go along with it just fine. Some even salivate when they see the syringe because a meal always follows. Thanks for loving this kitty. He's lucky to have you caring for him.

[**Note:** There are many reasons why a cat can become a diabetic, and sometimes it starts with overactive adrenal glands, a condition called Cushing's disease. The adrenals' job is to make cortisol (like cortisone). Adrenals that make too much cortisol will give continual big orders to a pancreas. That poor little pancreas then gets overworked and burned out. Thus, it fails to produce enough insulin. Sometimes a kitty's trouble begins with Cushing's disease, which damages her pancreas—and she ends up with diabetes, too.]

Excessive Sleeping

A grumpy, sleepy cat with fleas is also anemic and sick. Frontline should do the trick.

QUESTION:

My cat of eight months recently has been sleeping a lot, and every time I pick him up, he gets mad and bites me. My cat is normally very active, and doesn't mind getting handled. My cat right now is experiencing a lot of fleas. I don't know if that has to do with anything.

DR. NICHOL:

You make the diagnosis simple. Those fleas are a major nuisance to your cat and, in large numbers, will cause grumpiness. But more important, his fleas are sucking his blood and he may be getting anemic (low numbers of red blood cells). Anemia will cause weakness that might be responsible for his sleeping more. Lastly, not only is your grouchy cat biting you, I'll bet his fleas are as well. Are you getting sleepy and grumpy too?

Take this baby to the doctor. Have him examined to be sure that he doesn't have other problems in addition to fleas. Fleas have become hardy and adaptable while treatment has gotten more effective and easier. Ask for Frontline, a liquid that you "spot-on" on your cat just once a month. Nothing you can get at a pet supply store will come close to prescription treatments for your cat, your home, and your yard.

Postoperative Pain

Pets, without question, feel pain just as we do. Better pet hospitals treat and prevent pain.

QUESTION:

I have often wondered about cats and dogs and pain, especially when Skippy, our wonder cat with three legs, had most of his hind leg amputated to the hip. He came home the evening of surgery and my wife and I took turns holding him all night. He did not seem to be in pain, but rather out of it or a little crazy from the anesthetic. Isn't pain medication typically given for this kind of thing, and for such procedures as spaying a dog or cat? Don't the cats and dogs feel pain like we do after major surgery? We would certainly be given pain medication. What are your thoughts?

DR. NICHOL:

I am glad to get this question. There is a major move afoot among veterinary anesthesiologists to encourage greater use of the many pain relievers that are safe and effective for pets. But until the last several years, many of us didn't think very much about this important issue. We are not proud of this fact. Animals of all species, including humans, feel pain. But as many of us animal lovers often observe, our pets don't talk.

So, how do we know if and when pain management is necessary? If pets are like us, there are varying degrees of pain among individuals. How can we know when our treatment is sufficient? We are observant, that's how.

According to Dr. Robert Paddleford in his recent paper on analgesics, the signs to watch for are: increased heart or respiratory rate, unwillingness to move, drooling, poor appetite, restlessness, aggressive behavior, and crying (I think we already knew that one). Needless to say, some of these signs are vague. But pets who show two or three together definitely need our help. And we can choose from several drugs and methods of giving treatment.

Which is best? This is a great example of the adage that medicine is still more art than science. What is best for a pet is the pain management that is most familiar and safe in your veterinarian's experience. Different cases require different treatments. In our hospital, we use pain treatments before surgery. For procedures like spaying and neutering, that cause only mild discomfort, we use an injection of Torbugesic about one hour prior to anesthesia. The pet is relaxed as he or she goes to sleep and feels a whole lot better for up to five hours after recovery. If needed, the injection can be repeated. But for fracture surgery or an amputation for a pet like Skippy the Wonder Cat, we apply a Duragesic skin patch the day before surgery.

A pain patch is nifty. Using the same principle as the skin patches for people trying to quit smoking, they provide a continuous through-the-skin release of the drug for three to five days. We send the pet home wearing a patch and recheck the pet's comfort a few days later and replace the skin patch, if needed. This way no one has to give pills and the pain relief is continuous. Everybody's happier.

We welcome interest in pain relief. Let's face it—most injured pets will get well without help with pain. But we love these little guys like our children. Which of us would knowingly deny pain relief to a hurting child? But for us to help every pet with pain, we need observant pet owners. Be aware and be the voice for your pets. Alleviating the suffering of animals is a responsibility we all can share.

Stiff-Legged, Weak Cat

Low potassium causes poor muscle function. Get a thorough health evaluation to rule out other problems. The right supplement will make it right.

QUESTION:

Blinken is my 9-year-old cat and he's been acting funny lately. He's always been pretty healthy, but for the last few weeks he seems weak. He doesn't want to walk around the house much and, when he does, his legs are kind of stiff. But the part that I really noticed is that his head is down. He won't look up. What's wrong with Blinken?

DR. NICHOL:

Blinken has a serious problem—I'm glad you wrote in. You did not mention what diet you feed Blinken nor whether he goes outside. This is important because his symptoms could result from thiamine deficiency or poisoning from antifreeze or certain insecticides. But assuming that Blinken stays inside and that you feed him a decent diet, I would have to suspect low blood potassium. We call this feline hypokalemic polymyopathy or hypokalemia for short. While it can lead to death, the good news is that it is almost always manageable, although not curable.

Here's how it works. Hypokalemia occurs when the kidneys allow too much of the electrolyte potassium to slip out into the urine. Because potassium is important in the normal functioning of muscles, cats with this problem get weak and may walk with a stilted gait. They lack the strength to keep their heads up. To help Blinken, we first would need to check a blood sample to confirm our suspicions. If his potassium is very low, it would be corrected intravenously. If it's only moderately below normal, an oral supplement called Tumil-K should work fine. Tumil-K is a powder that is mixed with the food. Most cats don't seem to mind taking it. Because hypokalemia is a long-term problem, Blinken is likely to need Tumil-K for the rest of his life.

Can hypokalemia be prevented? Some cases can be. Not every cat with this disease is losing potassium through the kidneys. Low blood levels can also result from feeding a deficient diet. But don't bother to read the labels on the packages. Just know that deficient diets are cheap diets. When it comes to pet food, the good stuff costs a bit more. You don't get what you don't pay for. Besides, Blinken isn't a cheap cat anyway.

Excessive Drinking in Older Cats

Always a serious sign—move quickly. A thorough exam plus lab work may uncover age-related kidney failure, a disease that may be treatable.

QUESTION:

Our cat Bugsy is 17 years old and she seems to be acting like the years are catching up to her. For the past two or three weeks she's been drinking more water and she's hardly eating. My sister thinks her breath smells like urine, but I say it's because her teeth are bad. How could a cat's breath smell like urine?

DR. NICHOL:

You are right to be concerned about Bugsy. At age 17, there are several age-related problems that could cause her to drink more water and reduce her eating. Diseases to consider include kidney failure, thyroid tumors, diabetes, liver disease, and possibly cancer.

What about the urine smell to her breath? This is an astute observation on the part of your sister. This symptom is often seen in kidney failure in cats as well as in dogs. The reason is that worn-out, failing kidneys are falling way behind in their work. One of the important jobs they do is to eliminate what's called nitrogenous wastes (the stuff that gives urine its smell) from the body. When the kidneys are unable to handle that job, the body tries desperately to get rid of these wastes some other way. In Bugsy's case, her body is excreting some of it through the membranes of her mouth.

I know that it's hard to hear this news, but your Bugsy is a pretty sick old kitty. Her kidney failure is advanced. It is likely to have been going on for a long time. But please don't feel like you have neglected her. Symptoms like hers really do present themselves suddenly, even though her problem has been gradual in its development. While organ failure like this is a slow process, other organ systems are remarkable in their ability to compensate for the shortcomings in her kidneys. Finally, though, her system is starting to collapse.

Can we help Bugsy? It is possible. What you must do immediately is to get her to her doctor for an exam and some lab work. If her kidney failure is confirmed, but is not too severe, treatment with fluids intravenously and medications to manage her nausea and mouth pain may help a lot. If she responds well, she may do well at home for quite a while on a special diet and oral medications. Even at 17 she may still have a few good miles left on the clock. Whatever you do, don't allow this old friend to go any longer without help. Her poor appetite is caused by her nausea. She feels pretty bad.

By the way, for younger kitties whose kidneys have run into serious trouble, kidney transplants are available. Finding suitable donors is much easier than other species—any cat with the same blood type could be a kidney donor. They generally do well long term with easy-to-live-with antirejection medication.

Feline AIDS Can Cause Chronic Disease in Cats

Many different long-term symptoms can suggest AIDS. Infected kitties must be handled carefully to allow them to live as long and as well as possible.

QUESTION:

My cat Jessie has been sick on and off for a long time, so I got worried about him. He's had a snotty nose and a fever and then he starting losing weight. So I took him to the vet who did some blood tests and he came up AIDS positive. Now I'm really scared. Will Jessie die soon? What about my kids and me—are we going to get sick, too?

DR. NICHOL:

I know how worried you are. It's true that Jessie is a very sick kitty, but he may do OK for a while. Rest assured that you and you family are not at risk of getting AIDS from your cat. Not only has it never happened; it really can't. The virus that causes feline AIDS has no way of infecting people.

While people can't get AIDS from a cat, there are some striking similarities with the human disease. AIDS in cats is a lifelong disease, there is no vaccination against it yet, and while we can help an infected cat feel better, we can't cure it.

I know this is bad news for Jessie, but he could do well for quite a while with good supportive care. For example, with upper respiratory symptoms, like his nasal discharge, oral antibiotics can make a world of difference. To be sure the right antibiotic is used, a nasal culture will be important. In addition, if he is dehydrated and malnourished, fluids intravenously and feeding through a special P.E.G. tube could save his life. As long as the AIDS infection in his body is not in its terminal stages, he should respond very well.

While AIDS in cats is scary for us cat lovers, we could all do well with some good information. This infection is found all over the world. Infected male cats outnumber females 3 to 1 because the majority of infections are contracted through fight wounds; the virus is present in large numbers in the saliva. While other methods of transmission include lactation (kittens nursing from infected mother cats) and breeding, infections from these sources are rare.

When do we suspect AIDS in a sick kitty? Often the tipoff is signs of AIDS-related complex (ARC). This really just means chronic infections that have occurred for months or years—similar to what has happened to Jessie. This includes infections of the inside of the mouth, diarrhea, skin problems, urinary infections, anemias, weight loss, and respiratory infections like Jessie's. When a cat with AIDS gets real sick, weight loss becomes severe. In addition, they can also have behavioral changes like pacing, twitching, or hiding.

I know how horrible this sounds. Fortunately, we can spare a terminal cat the fear and indignity of a wretched death by humane injection. Know that you may be able to keep Jessie comfortable and happy for quite awhile. By taking the time to write to me with your question, you have helped increase public awareness of feline AIDS. The bottom line is this: Do your best to prevent feline AIDS by keeping your cats indoors. And neuter your male kitties to curb their desire to fight.

Complications in Infant Kittens

Problems develop fast. Learn to correct low blood sugar and hypothermia.

QUESTION:

My cat just had kittens two weeks ago and one died yesterday. I found him off by himself moving slowly and crying. It broke my heart.

I didn't know what to do for him. Any ideas? The other six kittens seem OK, but I'm worried that it might happen to another one.

DR. NICHOL:

That is so hard to take. The excitement of raising babies is great until you have a disaster. I will give you an understanding of what works in many cases.

First and most important, be sure not to blame yourself. There can be many reasons why young puppies and kittens die in the first few weeks. Sometimes there are birth defects, but infections, dehydration, and failure to take adequate nutrition are also common causes. In fact, only 70 percent of puppies and kittens survive to weaning age. But like most disease states, knowing how to recognize a problem early can make all the difference.

Here are the common early signs: Crying, slow activity, diarrhea, and isolation from the littermates. Once you notice any symptom like these, move quickly. Start by putting a small amount (4 to 6 drops) of 50:50 honey:water or Karo Syrup on the baby's gums. We do this because most sick babies under the age of 16 weeks have low blood sugar as part of the problem. Next, warm the little guy up. You can do this many ways, but what's best is to put the little rascal in your shirt right next to your skin or on no fewer than three layers of towel on a heating pad set on low. At this point, if he starts to move a little faster, you're on your way—but you must get some real food into that tiny tummy or his blood sugar will plummet even lower after that first dose wears off. The best real food for kittens is KMR; for puppies, it's Esbilac. Your veterinarian has them.

If the baby gets even more active, you can heave that big sigh of relief—but you still need one more thing from your veterinarian—a diagnosis. You need this because these things seldom happen all by themselves. If the cause is not corrected, it can occur again to the same kitten or to the entire litter.

There is nothing like saving a life. It's my favorite part of my job. But please don't feel badly about the kitten who died. You have learned to save another by asking for help.

Feline Infectious Peritonitis (FIP)

A contagious disease, it is always fatal. Our best success is help-ing some cats feel OK.

QUESTION:

My cat Roger is real sick. He's only about 1 year old and for the past three weeks he's not been very active, and not eating very much. I think he has a fever, too. Then his belly started to get kind of bloated looking. His doctor said that Roger might have FIP. Can we try antibi-otics?

DR. NICHOL:

I am sorry to hear about Roger's illness. He truly is quite sick. Unfortunately, while there are a few medications that could help Roger, antibiotics will only help a little. First, I will explain FIP.

FIP stands for feline infectious peritonitis. It is caused by a virus that is often transmitted to kittens by their mothers or by other adult cats. Cats at greatest risk are those who live in multiple-cat households or in breeding catteries. Kittens born in these groups are at greatest risk. The worst news of all is that FIP is a fatal disease. It causes a severe inflammation of blood vessels. It can affect many internal systems like the kid-neys, eyes, brain, and liver. But the symptoms most often seen are like those that Roger has; that is the effusive or "wet" form of FIP. "Effusive" means that fluid accumulates in the abdomen or chest causing a bloated tummy (like Roger's) or difficulty breathing (fluid in the chest). Although the fluid buildup is not usually painful, these kitties run fevers, feel badly, and have poor appetites.

What can we do for Roger? Since FIP is an inflammatory disease with involvement of a cat's immune system, drugs like prednisone, that suppress the immune response could help Roger to feel better and live longer. Drainage of the fluid in his belly and a blood transfusion will also help. Most of all, you need to prepare for losing Roger some day. I am sorry—FIP is not curable.

Lastly, there is a preventive for cats who are at risk. The FIP vaccine, which is given by nosedrops, is moderately effective. It is best started when kittens are 16 weeks old, then boostered three to four weeks later. Since we don't see much FIP, except in multiple-cat households and catteries, an average housecat has no real need for vaccination. On the other hand, purebred kittens purchased from breeding operations or pet stores should be tested right away to be sure they are free of the disease. Adult cats intended for breeding should be tested first, then vaccinated before being introduced into a group.

TRAVELING CATS

■■■■■■■■■■■■■■■■■■■■■■■■■■■■■

Car Travel and Frightened Cats

Dramamine or Acepromazine is helpful if used before the trip.

QUESTION:

A few years ago when I moved across country, my vet told me to sedate my cat by giving him half of a Dramamine tablet. I've since heard that this is not a good idea. I'm taking an extended vacation this spring and want to take my cats with me. Is it OK to give them the Dramamine?

DR. NICHOL:

Sure, your cats can have Dramamine. It's a safe and effective way to induce a stupor and prevent motion sickness. The dose is 12.5 milligrams every eight hours. Just break the over-the-counter 50-milligram pill into quarters. Start the trip by giving one-quarter tablet about 30 minutes before hopping into the car. That's because it works a lot better as a preventive. If a cat is already on the road and upset, it's not likely to work. Feel better now? Good. Please don't take Dramamine yourself before traveling. It doesn't matter if you get carsick and vomit; we just don't want an unsafe driver with cats onboard.

To Drive or Fly . . . That Is the Question

How does your cat relate to the carrier?

QUESTION:

I have two Abyssinian cats. We're moving, but I'm not sure if we're going to fly—which would take about six hours—or drive, which would take four or five days. I was wondering which way would be better to transport my cats and what means would we use to move them for each (i.e., I heard that you tranquilize the cat to fly)?

DR. NICHOL:

I don't think tranquilizing a cat to fly will work. I've tranquilized lots of cats and not one has ever taxied down a runway and . . . Oh well, maybe that's not what you meant anyway.

Traveling with cats: You can go either way. If these cats are calm inside a carrier crate on car rides, I would send them by air and get the trip over quickly for them. On the other hand, if they are frightened and noisy in the car, they will absolutely panic in the plane. So, if they're bad riders in the car, my best advice is to drive them—and tranquilize them. Get a tranquilizer called Acepromazine from your veterinarian and use it liberally while driving. (On the cats, that is.) Dramamine works fine, too. (See previous question and answer.)

While the car trip is longer, you will have the peace of mind of having your kitties with you. You can comfort them and repeat the tranquilizer tablets as needed. But, you don't want them to freak out in the baggage compartment of the plane. Even with tranquilizers, they can get pretty scared if they are all alone.

URINARY DISEASE

Recurrent Urinary Disease

Cats with frequent bouts of painful straining to urinate can find relief—but an accurate diagnosis is needed first.

QUESTION:

I have a Maine Coon cat who is over 8 years old. She is very prone to urinary tract infection. My vet has her on special foods as well as Methigel. She gets better, then flares up again within a few days. Is there any cure? What will be the long-term effects for my cat? I need help desperately.

DR. NICHOL:

Yes, this disease is curable in most cases. Your kitty's problem is that there is another, yet undiscovered, cause for her symptoms. The other causes include feline leukemia infection, feline AIDS, bacterial infection, or stones inside her bladder. In rare cases, there can be cancers or malformations of the wall of the bladder. Ask your cat's doctor to culture her urine and do blood testing for leukemia and AIDS. X-rays of her bladder and possibly an ultrasound examination will also be helpful in uncovering the cause(s). Most important: Do not give up. Your cat is miserable. If left unmanaged, her problem could progress to a blockage of the outflow of her urine. This could end up fatal.

Frequent Urinations

Frequent attempts to urinate may signal serious disease. Do the right thing first.

QUESTION:

I have a 12-year-old male cat who has a bladder infection and it is not getting better even with antibiotics. I see him going to the litter box all day long. In our backyard, he has dug little holes where I see him urinating or at least trying to. After he uses the litter box, he drops blood all over the house. I don't know what else to do other than to put him to sleep because I know he must be in pain. He has lost a lot of weight and seems to cry all night long.

DR. NICHOL:

This sounds just miserable. I completely understand that you want to end his suffering. But please don't have him put to sleep. I think we can put him right.

Your kitty has what we call feline lower urinary tract disease. It's an inflammatory problem that causes thickening and sometimes bleeding of the bladder wall. Infection is responsible for only about 3 percent of these problems. Many are caused by a combination of crystals and mucus that can block the flow of urine. The bottom line: Your kitty may be unable to empty his bladder. He's in constant pain.

Have him tested for feline leukemia and feline AIDS virus. If he's negative, he'll need a urinalysis and culture as well as X-rays of his bladder. His weight loss worries me, so I would also check a blood pressure, blood count, and chemistry profile to look for kidney damage. It's time we fill in the blanks in this boy's health.

He may need a different antibiotic; but if he can't pass urine, he may also need surgery. In males, the urethra (the tube that carries urine from the bladder) narrows as it passes through the penis. Many urinary blockages occur at this location. Surgical correction will provide a wider urethra that will allow crystals to pass normally and painlessly. But if his long-standing disease is in the bladder wall, he may only get the relief he needs from antiinflammatory and antispasmodic medications. In addition, the anti-anxiety drug amitriptyline may also be helpful. The good news is that we know more now than ever about how to help a cat like this. Don't give up. Invest whatever it takes to give him his health back.

Repeated Bouts of Inability to Urinate

Kidney damage and severe pain mark these repeated episodes. Surgery of the penis and urethra can be the best way to assure quality of life.

QUESTION:

I live in Japan and recently, for the fourth time, my male Siamese was not able to urinate. The doctor has shown me the fine crystals found in his urine when he was forcibly voided. The fourth time, about two weeks ago, the doctor couldn't dislodge the crystals from his urinary tract and had to put him out and clear the tubes. The cat, Puyi, is 5 years and 4 months old. He eats everything including a steady diet of sewer rats when he can catch them. I have looked at different books in English and some say this is caused by too rich a diet; others say it is caused by ash and magnesium and my doctor says it is caused by too much salt and has given me Science Diet's s/d formula. The vet also said cats with this do not live past middle age.

I wish to know if it is just diet and what can I do about it? Puyi gets four to five Pounce treats a night. Besides a proper diet, I love my pet very much, but I am wondering how much medical treatment I can afford to give him. I have spent $350.00 this month and dread to think of future costs and yet, think I will do anything for him. He is a loving wonderful pet with a perky and friendly personality—the life of the neighborhood. Children are starving all over the world, do I spend hundreds, even thousands on him? Is it myself that I am spending the money on? There are two separate issues here: actual diet and health care; and the psychological guilt I feel even wondering about money. Any words of advice and encouragement will be most welcome.

Dr. Nichol:

You have raised several important issues; some medical, some quite personal. The emotional distress you are feeling is the essence of why we have pets in our lives. You have struck to the very center of the love and caring felt by my readers and me. Without the gift of unconditional love from cats like Puyi and the joy felt in giving it back, there would be no knowledge of problems like feline urinary disease. No one would have bothered to discover its treatment.

Now that we're clear on why you spent the time to write, let's fix poor Puyi. The sudden inability of some male cats to pass urine results from a mixture of crystals and mucus in the urine. There are several reasons why it happens almost exclusively in male cats. The first reason is chemical. The crystals that cause the blockage are composed of mineral salts called struvite. There are three primary ions involved, but the most important is magnesium. Diets low in this mineral (but still providing the trace amounts required for normal health) help prevent the problem. Another reason is anatomical. Female cats have short wide urethras (the tube that carries urine from the bladder to the outside). If a female cat makes crystals, she is unlikely to even know it because they simply pass right through. That's because the crystals rarely stick together to form a stone like in people and dogs. But the problem in male cats is their narrow urethras. With their smaller passageway, the crystals can form a plug and suddenly the poor guy can pass only a few drops of urine or none at all. Without immediate treatment, death can be imminent.

There is no doubt that Puyi's doctor did the right thing. By getting that plug of crystals out of the urethra, Puyi's plumbing could start to function normally again. But why does this keep happening to this little fellow? Each time Puyi has gotten a blockage of his urethra, he has been left with more inflammation and scarring. The result is a more narrow urethra, making it even easier for clumps of struvite crystals to block his urine flow. Each time Puyi can't urinate, he has tremendous pain and back pressure on his kidneys. Much more of this and he won't get past middle age because his kidneys will fail. What he needs is serious prevention.

Tell the doctor that you want an operation called a perineal urethrostomy for Puyi. It is essential because it will remodel his urethra, resulting in a short wide passageway like that of a female cat. It's also important to continue the s/d food in that it will help reduce formation of more crystals. Lastly, and this goes for *all* indoor cats, provide several fresh unused litter pans. Cats have a much better sense of smell than we have. In addition, they are very clean creatures. Even if his litter pan smells OK to you, if it has been used at all you are asking your cat to step around in a stinky soggy mess. Many cats would rather hold their urine than face this indignity. That stagnating urine in their bladders greatly increases the risk of urinary disease. Oh, and the Pounce treats and sewer rats—no problem. Like a glass of good scotch, they are fine if taken in moderation.

It is very clear from your letter that you love your cat with intensity. This is not only OK—it is part of what makes you a healthy and loving person. Puyi helps bring out your best. Love is the reason we are in this life. Invest whatever resources you must to ensure his long life. If you draw the line on Puyi's value, you are also limiting what you bring to others. Yes, children are starving. But if spending less on Puyi could save them, we should all forego everything but food and water. All else is luxury. Spending less on our pets won't reduce world hunger.

Everyday we create wealth both emotional and monetary. It is not a finite thing. Follow your heart.

Kidney Transplants

A highly successful way to save the life of a beloved cat with failed kidneys.

QUESTION:

What can you tell me about the success of feline kidney transplants? One of my cats has been diagnosed with chronic renal failure, and my wife and I are considering renal transplantation. We would like to know the best clinics or schools of veterinary medicine to contact.

DR. NICHOL:

What once sounded bizarre and impossible is today not only feasible, but highly successful. Cats who are in otherwise good health can be fairly easily matched with suitable donors and go on to live normal happy lives.

Interesting, isn't it? Here is how it works. Unlike most other species, the feline immune system can avoid rejection of donated organs as long as both cats share the same blood type. Following successful transplant surgery, the recipient must take the immune suppressant drug Cyclosporine for life. That's because while blood type assures a close match, it's never perfect. The drug is safe, relatively inexpensive, and given at home in pill form.

But while this surgery enjoys great success, it's highly specialized. Two veterinary teaching institutions carry out the procedure: The University of California at Davis and The University of Florida. Since the system was developed first and is carried out in greater numbers at Davis, this may be the better hospital for your kitty.

Cool, huh? Actually it's truly fortunate that the Maker gave each of us two kidneys. Cats, in particular, have a high rate of kidney disease and kidney failure. Each of us has plenty of function in just one normal kidney to carry us for a lifetime. So a kitty with two bad ones can be saved with a donation of just one kidney from another cat—usually a healthy stray from animal control. That means that the donor can also go on to enjoy a normal life expectancy. Thus, the last requirement is for the family to adopt that homeless donor cat. You feel great love for your pets. If I were a cat on death row I'd be the first to volunteer when the call came.

URINATION AND DEFECATION BEHAVIORS

Litter Box Problem 1:
Pooping Outside the Pan

Learn the ways of the feline and master the problem.

QUESTION:

I have an 8-year-old male Russian Blue cat. I clean out the box every day. My "Gray Boy" will poop on the carpet in my living room, and on the bathroom floors. It is very frustrating. He is in good health, and there has not been any changes in the house, physically or emotionally. Yet he is doing this deliberately and for no apparent reason. My vet can give me no other explanation for this rude behavior.

DR. NICHOL:

Whoever said cats were delicate and fastidious creatures? Not me. Oh, yeah, it was me. But I wasn't talking about your cat and, come to think of it, I wasn't talking about mine either. Hmmm. Must have been a cat I met in a previous life. But I will commend you for doing a lot right.

Your kitty may have an aversion to the types of litters you've tried or to the location of the pan; or he may have a physical reason such as impacted anal glands, chronic constipation, or abdominal pain. Start by asking his doctor to repeat his physical exam with special emphasis on these possibilities. Bring a fresh stool sample (not in short supply at your house) so that this juvenile delinquent can be checked for intestinal parasites. If all of the above is fine, we'll move on to the next space on the gameboard—behavioral issues.

So why do some cats do this? He isn't being rude on purpose; he's a cat and cats can be like that anyway. It's happening because this guy has bathroom preferences built right into his little brain. On top of those preferences, he has developed bad habits that are becoming more deeply engrained with each passing day. Act decisively. Get a few more litter pans (no roofs, vents or filters, please) and put them on the places where Gray Boy has defecated. Use a different type of litter in each. Your options include clumping, clay, Yesterday's News (pelleted, recycled newspaper), fine-grade playground sand, and no. 3 blasting sand. Try filling the pans to varying depths. If you carry out this experiment methodically, you are likely to determine the exact preference of this sociopath. If you still have trouble, let me know and we'll discuss making it a negative experience for him to practice pooping in prohibited places.

Is this fun or what? Actually, if clumping litter works out well, consider getting a Litter Maid—a self-cleaning pan. We have one at our animal hospital. You never handle the used litter and your cat always has a fresh pan. Besides, watching the Litter Maid work is cheap entertainment.

Litter Box Problem II: Urinating Outside the Pan

Behavior management is the key.

QUESTION:

I have an 8-year-old female Siamese cat who has chosen to urinate on a chair or bed—always in the same places. I have covered them with plastic, but she still does it. She has always been an uptight cat. She knows this is inappropriate behavior because she will run and hide. I have tried punishment, ignoring, anything else I can think of. I took her to the vet who found her in perfect physical condition and ordered Prozac, which is not working. I realize this is probably "spite," but I give her a lot of attention and she has been doing this for five years with an increase as time goes on. It seemed to start at the time of my divorce. Please help—I'm at my wits' end!

Dr. Nichol:

I'm glad you wrote in. It's when people are at their "wits' end" that I know they are desperate enough to follow a whole new method of behavior management. Correcting your cat's urination habits will require patience and time.

I will begin by reminding you of the big reason some folks find it easier to love pets than people. The love we get from our critters is pure. In other words, forget about spite. Honest. I've had a bunch of formal training and a heap of experience in managing and preventing behavior problems in pets. They are like us in many ways, but unlike us (in fact, better than us) in a few others. So why does she act guilty? Because she knows that you'll be angry when you find the urine, but she has this darn habit and she doesn't know how to stop. Now you're both unhappy. Here's how to both get happy.

First, get rid of the odor. While household cleaners can reduce the smell so that you don't notice it, your cat still does. Get a product called Equalizer or Outright. These liquids have no smell. They work because they contain an active organism that literally consumes the organic matter from the urine. Use it exactly as the label instructs. Next, make that chair and bed really weird places to urinate by laying a sheet of aluminum foil over them. If you want to really spoil the fun, put a Scat Mat over them.

But this is only the start. If we don't help your kitty change her behavior, she'll just do the same thing some other place. Manage this by providing her a totally fresh, unused litter pan at all times. It's easy. Just keep three or four pans each with a small amount of cheap fresh litter. Check the pans twice a day.

Dump, rinse, and replace the litter in any that have been used. If she always has access to a fresh litter box, she will prefer that.

Last, but not least, think about your poor uptight kitty's being so darn uptight. Remember that it was a major change in your home (your husband leaving) that got her wigged out in the first place. To get her to relax and accept life a little better, you have a few choices: (1) you could take your husband back, (2) you could take Prozac yourself and you wouldn't care that your cat is uptight, or (3) you could give her a drug called Buspar for one to two months. The correct answer is (3) because Buspar is an effective anti-anxiety drug for cats that works especially well for this problem.

Litter Box Problem III: Half In, Half Out
Litter Maid may be the solution.

QUESTION:

I have a cat I adopted from the pound. She's several years old and spayed. She's a good cat except for her bathroom habits. She gets in the litter box except for her rear end. Needless to say her "business" is outside the box. Help!

DR. NICHOL:

We've all heard the expression "Think outside the box," but to get your kitty to think inside the litter box, we must first understand why she doesn't just jump right in with her whole self and make a commitment.

Cats are fussy. They won't scratch and relieve themselves just anywhere. When outside, they select that perfect place with great care. I believe they see this process as an art form. Indoor cats are really outdoor cats who live indoors. The aversion this girl feels for the litter is shown by her unwillingness to settle into it and get comfortable. Your mission, should you decide to accept it, is to provide this little princess with the perfect bathroom.

Start by keeping her pan purrrfectly clean at all times. Forget the deodorizing crystals. Products meant to pass the human smell test mean nothing to cats. Your girl has a sense of smell that's ten times as acute as ours. Like her outdoor-living counterparts, your cat needs a fresh place to go every time. Your assignment is to experiment using a few pans each with different types of litter. When you learn which is her favorite, experiment again with different depths of litter in each pan. Once you gain her favor, you can also provide her with two identical pans, as she may prefer a different one for each bathroom function.

Too much work? I'll make it simple. Try clumping litter; the finer, softer stuff is most often preferred. To make life easier yet, use it in a Litter Maid—a self-cleaning litter pan. This is also safer if you have a dog. Litter pans are a cornucopia of special "dog treats." Those who indulge in this gourmet delicacy with clumping litter can get a horrible intestinal blockage.

The Clean-up Challenge

Here are some products to use—and how.

QUESTION:

We recently put in new carpet a month ago and by doing a "sniff test" have discovered one of my two cats, Bill or Hillary, has been urinating on it. I am very interested in the products you listed and would like to know where I can purchase either of them. Then is it OK to shampoo it after it has been treated?

DR. NICHOL:

For the odor eliminators, Equilizer or Outright, check with your veterinarian or with a pet supply dealer. Or you can call Foster and Smith, a mail-order house, at 800-562-7169 to order these or a Scat Mat. Remember that while these products are useful, they are only part of managing the cat who has forgotten where the bathroom is. Also be sure to provide plenty of fresh unused litter in several locations.

Regarding your question about shampooing the carpet. Yes, do it after you have eliminated the odor. If you shampoo first, you will only dilute and spread out the organic matter in the carpet, making it more difficult to eliminate. If you plan to bathe your cats, I say go ahead with that, too—just try to avoid getting a lot of hair stuck to your tongue.

The Cat Who Wet a Roommate's Bed

A cat can be a very bad ambassador of goodwill. It takes work, but it can be managed.

QUESTION:

My daughter's cat, April, is urinating on furniture. She has been fixed and is an indoor cat. She's been doing this since she moved in with new roommates over a year ago. She especially does this on her roommate's bed. She also acts a little "crazy" at times. What do you think is wrong? My daughter is desperate as she is considering giving up the cat.

DR. NICHOL:

It does my heart good to know that April means enough for you to ask for advice. Since this behavior started with the move (and those new roommates—hiss!!), it's pretty clear that April has responded badly to change.

First, here is what is *not* going on: April is not demonstrating her negative feelings toward the roommate by urinating on her bed. Cats and people do have some emotions in common, but we are not identical. Only humans are low enough for that kind of dirty trick. Why would a cat do such a disgusting thing? Because when a cat urinates someplace other than a litter pan, she is marking that thing as her territory. So, if that's the case, why is she still doing this over a year later? Because yet another nuance of cat behavior is the habit of returning to the same scent to urinate again. And the more she is allowed to repeat this behavior, the more ingrained it becomes. So we need to stop it soon.

Your mission, should you decide to accept it: Prevent April from having access to the roommate's bedroom. Also, provide at least three litter pans, always keeping them in the same places. Use only a small amount of litter in each pan and check them twice daily. Anytime you find one that has been used, dump it, rinse it with water, then replace with a small amount of litter. This will make the litter pans more appealing to her. To discourage her from urinating in the same bad places, start by eliminating the odor of past urine with Outright or Equilizer. Then lay aluminum foil on those spots. Lastly, get a prescription for Buspar from your veterinarian. This will help her abandon old anxieties.

The Untrained Kitty
There's probably a way to make him litter literate.

QUESTION:

Our new tabby, Pata Grande, has turned into a most loving kitten. Pata was not trained by his mother as a kitten to use a litter pan before being abandoned. Phoo Phoo, the senior animal and 12-year-old cat, is litter trained, but is not about to teach him. How do we train this newest member of our household to use the litter pan?

DR. NICHOL:

Cats really can't be litter trained; it's a behavior that develops in kittenhood. But you can encourage it by taking Pata Grande to the litter pan often, waiting for him to make you proud, and then throwing a party. Something like an inaugural bash will do nicely. When you catch him going in the wrong place, you can startle him with a handheld foghorn, but you must be quick—do it just as he is beginning the vile act in the wrong place.

So what if this fails? Plan B. Confine Pata to a restricted area and continue to encourage his bid for the presidency each time he exhibits good bathroom behavior. As he improves his litter box performance, you can expand his access to the rest of the house. Do this gradually. It takes a village to raise a kitten.

Habits of an Unspayed Cat

If your female cat holds her hind end in a funny position, don't shrug it off.

QUESTION:

My 5-year-old female cat has been urinating everywhere for the past six months. She has not been spayed, she always stays inside. She has lost some weight, but is very playful, runs, and plays with the dog. She doesn't act sick. She eats about the same as always. However, she's starting to hold her hind end funny. I hope you can help me.

DR. NICHOL:

Being unspayed and holding her hind end funny are likely to be related. In other words, your little girl is about to go into heat and develop a social life that could make you a grandparent. Regarding her "urinating everywhere," this may be behavioral or it may be a sign of important physical disease. Start by getting her examined by her doctor. Have a urinalysis and urine culture done to rule out infection or other bladder disease.

Cats Defecating in Flowerbeds and in the Children's Sandbox

Aluminum foil will foil the cats. But give them their own outdoor litter pan.

QUESTION:

We have two acres of property, yet our cats insist on using our flowerbeds and the children's sandbox (they have a lid, but sometimes the kids forget to put it down) for the potty. I have tried commercial preparations, mothballs, and red pepper mixed with mustard (not in the sandbox) to keep them out. We even dumped some kitty litter at a "good location" in a far corner. Do you know of any way to redirect them?

DR. NICHOL:

This is an important problem for a couple of reasons. First, it's disgusting. Second, and even more important, it's a possible health risk because intestinal parasites from your cats can infect your children. Are your cats trying to tell you something? Do they secretly resent you for giving your human children more expensive gifts than they get? Are they plotting escapades that are so evil that pooping in the sandbox pales in comparison? Naw. They don't even care what you think. They just think your flowerbeds and sandbox are interesting outdoor litter pans. And two more things: These places now smell like latrines to your cats and this aberrant pooping has become a habit.

Let's fix this bizarre bathroom behavior. You already understand the concept. Not only must we make the wrong locations undesirable poop places, we must also give your kitties a new lavatory that they will like even better. First, get rid of the odor of urine and stool by replacing the soil in your flowerbeds as well as the sand in the sandbox. This is important because cats have a superior sense of smell. Besides, they won't be fooled by products like Cat-B-Gone and mothballs. (Your cats are insulted that you think they resemble moths— they eat moths.) Next, make sure the sandbox stays covered when not in use. Make the flowerbeds unfun by laying aluminum foil on the dirt. (Cats do not like urinating on foil as their outfits might get mussed.) Then provide them a new outdoor litter box. I suggest a simple wood-frame box filled with the original dirt from the flowerbeds. This way the new litter box will feel and smell like the flowerbeds used to. When they start using this new bathroom, you can gradually drag it farther out into the back 40.

Sorry it's so hard. Don't lose your patience and try to correct their habits with squirt guns or land mines. It won't work and they'll only retaliate. Cats are cunning. You have no idea of the creative locations they can find if they really want to. It could get ugly.

Vaccinations

Vaccinations for Solo Kitties

Some vaccines may be less important for cats without exposure to other cats.

Question:

I have chosen not to vaccinate my indoor cat. I take my cat outside in the backyard a couple times a day while he is supervised by me every minute.

From the research I have done I don't think there is any chance of him getting feline leukemia or rabies, but I need to know about the four diseases that are contained within the feline distemper vaccine, which are rhinotracheitis, panleukopenia, chlamydia, and calicivirus/herpesvirus. Are these airborne viruses, and if so, is there much chance of my cat catching any of these while he is outside? How long can the virus survive in the air? Can the viruses get into dirt or flies or mosquitoes or even other animals' urine or feces?

Dr. Nichol:

You are asking some educated questions. Let's start with the basics. Vaccines work by stimulating the immune system with a virus that, in most cases, is more of a distant cousin than the true infectious organism. What results is the production of protein complexes called antibodies that will glom onto the virus itself if it ever finds its way inside the body. This concept of customizing somebody's defense system is pretty remarkable, but it may have a down side. These vaccines contain a variety of components that can cause allergic reactions and sometimes cancers.

With risks like that, who would bother? Well, let's face it; every day we all take risks. Just getting into your car is a gamble. But for the very small risk attendant to vaccinating we can drastically reduce the chances of death due to infectious disease.

OK, your cat is extremely unlikely to ever confront these ugly bugs, right? Well, let me say this about that. Consider the stray ally cat. Not only has he never had a vaccination, he can't even spell veterinarian. (Not to be confused with vegetarian, which is a plant doctor.) Believe it or not, feral cats rarely if ever get sick from contagious disease. That's because of the frequent "natural boostering" they get in small doses each time they share a cigarette or wine bottle with a colleague on a street corner. These guys are almost bulletproof. Your boy, on the other hand, is downright vulnerable. If his immune system never gets a stimulus of any kind, i.e., by vaccination or "natural exposure," he could get sick and die quite easily with a minor exposure. Even if you take full charge of his social calendar, he could need hospitalization for an unrelated illness and get exposed. In a weakened state he would succumb fast.

Which vaccines are most important? Start with rabies. It's a human disease, too, and failure to vaccinate could get you busted by Animal Control. For safety, make sure he gets a killed vaccine. The vaccine risk is close to zero. Next are the combination of panleukopenia (feline distemper) and the upper respiratory viruses. I vote yes to these because without them he is a sitting duck if he has even the slightest exposure. Feline leukemia: It's unnecessary for your cat. He would need to get bitten by an infected cat or share a home with one. Leukemia, by the way, is the vaccination with the greatest risk of causing cancer.

How vulnerable is your boy when he's taking a stroll in your yard? Not at all. While the upper respiratory bugs are airborne, they only pass over a distance of a few feet. They die quickly and don't persist in the environment. None of these organisms are present in stool or urine in enough numbers to be a risk in the soil. Mosquitoes are not a factor. But someday, outside the safety of your yard, this fellow may meet a virus that could hit him like a Mack truck. Make sure he has a crash helmet. Protection is good.

Vaccinations for Puppies and Kittens
What they really need and what's unnecessary.

QUESTION:

My kids, my wife, and I decided that we want to have a pet, but we can't agree on a dog or a cat—so we got both. We know they need shots, but I've called a few vet clinics and I'm getting different answers on how many shots they need. Can you advise us on what's best?

DR. NICHOL:

Boy, am I glad to hear this question. It is painful for me to recall the number of these babies who have died of preventable diseases only because their owners assumed they were too young to vaccinate. The reasons for the different answers to your questions result from different types of vaccine as well as the dated information that's included with the vaccine itself.

Let's start with the kitties. The best vaccine is a combination against panleukopenia, feline viral rhinotracheitis, and calici virus (FVR-C-P). Ideally this protection is started at 6 to 9 weeks of age. The combination vaccine is given a total of three times with an interval of about three weeks between each booster. At the time of the last vaccine, the one rabies vaccine is given. Cats are boostered annually after that. Now for the confusing part. There are combinations that contain a few additional vaccines. Many folks, including some veterinarians, feel that when it comes to vaccines, the more the merrier. But there is skepticism among specialists in internal medicine and immunology. Many experts feel that if a young puppy or kitten does not have an exposure risk to some of these less common diseases, the extra vaccine may do more harm than good. This is because more vaccine or "antigenic load" given at the same time can overwhelm the immune system, thus reducing that youngster's response to the other, more important vaccines. On the other hand, if your kitten will be spending a lot of time outside with other neighborhood cats, protection against feline leukemia will be important. But, again, it is much better in the babies not to include the leukemia vaccine with the others, but instead to give it as a series of two injections after the regular series is finished. A blood test for the leukemia virus is useful first to make sure that your new kitten is not already infected. (This can happen to the litter of kittens while they are still in the uterus.)

For your new puppy: The biggest difference in vaccines is the parvo component of the distemper–parvo combination (DA2PPL). Many vaccines still in use contain low-titer parvo vaccine. But the newer high-titer vaccines are much better because they stimulate an immunity faster and with greater reliability. While the insert that is shipped with some vaccines recommends longer series, independent research has clearly shown that most puppies get a reliable protection with a series of three high-titer DA2PPL vaccinations starting at 6 to 9 weeks of age. Space the vaccines about three weeks apart.

What happens if you give more in a series "just to be safe"? Infectious disease specialists feel that by overloading the immune system this way, we may actually be setting up some puppies for immune-mediated disease later in life. They point out that vaccines are necessary for protection, but they can be harmful if overused.

Lastly, there are additional vaccines available for puppies. These include corona virus, bordatella, and Lyme disease. Some puppies will need these, but most will not. Adding them in all together, however, can reduce the effectiveness of the distemper and parvo components that are most important. If additional vaccines like these are needed, it is best to give them separately at the end of the series. When we see the puppy for his or her last booster, we give the one rabies vaccine; then we repeat the vaccinations once yearly after that.

Can these vaccines fail? There is a rare puppy or kitten who fails to fully respond. But by far the most common cause of so-called vaccination failure occurs with vaccinations purchased by mail or from pet supply stores. Is it because it's bad vaccine, administered incorrectly, or stored improperly? Hard to say. But when it comes to the protection of an important family member, saving money on vaccinations could cost a life. Protect those new babies and keep them safe.

How to Choose the Right Veterinarian

Aren't all veterinarians trained alike? If they give good service and have convenient hours, isn't that enough?

Well, sorry. All veterinarians are not created equal. But deep down inside, you already know that. In fact, if you're interested enough in the well-being of your pets to read this book, I'm sure you're going to be thinking about who you'd like to have for your veterinarian.

I could be glib in addressing this question. It would be simple to say, "Pick me." I am a good veterinarian. I've been at it a long time (I graduated from the College of Veterinary Medicine at Michigan State University in 1974). I take more than twice the required continuing education that my state requires for licensure. I'm conscientious and I communicate well. I have a great support staff, and everyone on that staff cares deeply about pets. And I'm an advocate of thorough preventive, diagnostic, and treatment techniques. I am single-minded about giving the best health care to every pet. I don't know any other way.

But . . . would I be perfect for you and your pets? Well, maybe. To be honest, there's more to this choice than just checking out my qualifications.

I'm a firm believer in excellent, healthy relationships. I also believe that if you want a specific type of service and you are willing to pay for it, you ought to get it. Toward this end I will provide you with a list of qualifications and considerations that good veterinarians satisfy. Then I will help you evaluate the "short list."

Having said all that, I will not be so presumptuous as to assume that you want the same things in a veterinarian as I think best. While you love your pets, you may not want to invest your hard-earned paycheck in procedures like advanced dental treatments, endoscopic biopsies, ultrasound, or electrocardiography—and that's OK with me. We live in a free market economy, and I believe you have a legitimate choice. But here's what I would do if I were in your shoes, trying to figure out the best doctor for a favorite pet: Break it down into a couple of simple components.

There are two steps. First, make sure your veterinarian-to-be meets a list of objective criteria that you can quickly and easily research. Second, have some face-to-face contact with the contestants who reach the finals. Sort of like an interview with a few of the Miss America Finalists. Shucks, this is getting exciting.

So whip out the Yellow Pages and flip to V. Look for the following in the listing—or call the best prospects and ask a few questions. Here are the topics worth covering:

1. *The AAHA logo.* If you're like most pet owners, you've never heard of this. It stands for American Animal Hospital Association. This is a lot more than a club. It is not mandatory for a hospital to join. While membership is open to all animal hospitals, only those adhering to stringent voluntary requirements and inspections are allowed to display the AAHA logo. It is expensive. But veterinarians who are serious about quality invest the money and energy to pass. These are the good guys. Only 15 percent of animal hospitals qualify.

2. *More than one doctor in the practice.* At least three is best. Why? Because, as Confucius said, "None of us is as smart as all of us." The best doctors don't need to be asked to get a second opinion for their clients. At a good hospital, anything that is not clear cut warrants a consultation. Buy one opinion, get two more free.

3. *"Closed for lunch?"* What the heck does that mean? Closed for *lunch*?? So if your pet gets hit by a car at 12:15, the people at the veterinary hospital need to finish their pie a la

mode before they can come to the rescue? I don't think so. You need a veterinarian whenever your pet does.

4. *Extended hours.* A hospital that's open 24 hours is great, but few are. Many are open until 7 P.M. or later, as well as every day of the week. Very few pet health problems have to be treated right now. But there are a lot of times when you'll want to see the doctor sometime before the end of the day. Besides, the convenience of evening and weekend appointments is, well, a convenience.

5. *"By appointment only?"* Red flag! What is this? We'll see your pet on our terms? Take a number? Get in line? If your pet is sick enough to need help, you want to be able to come in now. (A word of advice, though: When a problem crops up, and you need to take your pet in right away, better call ahead. Most hospitals don't have a clairvoyant on staff.)

6. *Services you want.* For instance, if the ad for the veterinarian says spays, neuters, and vaccinations and that's about it, you won't be happy. "Wellness only"-type clinics will refer anything else to a general practice. I recommend looking for a broad range of services such as cancer treatment, dental care, illness, and injury. Better yet: Look for an ad that lists behavior management, too. Try to get most of what you may need under one roof.

7. *Proximity to home.* This is by far the most common criterion used by folks searching for a new veterinarian. It makes sense in case of emergency, but don't rank convenience over quality.

Okay, have you found one or two that pass the above that are located in the same hemisphere as your home? Now for the warm and fuzzy part: If you're going to entrust the health of your beloved pet to this stranger, you'll need to get beyond the stranger thing. The process of meeting and sizing up the doctor, staff, and the facility will tell you volumes about how people- and pet-friendly they are. To that goal do these things:

1. Call the clinic and tell the receptionist that you are looking for a veterinary hospital and that you'd like to stop by and meet one of the doctors and take a tour of the facility. Ask when would be a good time. Let the receptionist know that you plan to bring your pet.

2. Show up a few minutes early and look around the reception room. Is it clean or does it stink? Presentation counts. Do the folks at the desk wear clean uniforms? Do they smile? Are they polite? Every one of these things translates directly into how attuned to detail the whole operation is. Those little things matter.

3. Observe the manner of the staff regarding your request. Do they act like it's the goofiest thing anyone has ever asked—to meet the folks and take a tour? If so, I would feign acute abdominal distress and exit gracefully.

4. Do they say hello to your pet? I hope they like pets and that they're not afraid to show it. So they're genuinely nice people, happy to have you there. They want you to feel comfortable. That's what you want.

5. Ask a couple of questions. What happens to severely sick or injured pets? Is there a policy for quick handling of urgent cases? The providers of customer service will tell you much more than the doctor. That's because most doctors know how they want their support staff to behave. But not all of us know how to motivate people to do it. So ask at the desk and you'll learn what truly does happen.

6. If you're waiting for a long time (more than 20 minutes), does anyone get back to you to explain the delay? Do they offer you a drink? (Not a cocktail, I mean something like water or soda pop.)

7. When the doctor invites you into the exam room, does he or she introduce him- or herself? Is the doctor rushed? A harried doctor makes more mistakes. A good organization has composed professionals.

8. Does the doctor say hello to your pet? Friendly is good.

9. Ask the doctor how he or she handles a case that is outside his or her area of expertise. Wait for the doctor to say that there is a specialist in most cases who will take referrals. If it's clear that this veterinarian knows his or her limitations, you have a winner. Nobody knows it all. There is just way too much to be known for anyone to specialize in everything.

10. Ask the good doctor if he or she has an area of special interest or skill. Each of us should have one or a few areas of medicine that really turn us on. If this doctor has nothing in particular that gets his or her juices flowing, I would feel underserved.

11. The tour: Do they show you everything? How about the area where the cages and runs are? Are they spacious and clean or does it look and smell more like the "back room"? At our place I tell my staff that our hospital ward is the most important room. If our greatest priority is the pets who are the sickest, then we had better give them the very best. If they're going to get well, they need it to be clean and comfortable.

So the tour is over and the staff seemed glad that you and your pet came. Do they seem like the kind of folks who would help you whenever you had a problem? How about if you called the third or fourth time about dispensed medication? Maybe you were so flustered that you were *still* confused about the directions on the bottle. Would they be caring and understanding? If the answers to most of the above is yes, then I think you just hit pay-dirt. Sign up.

The Risk of a Low-Fee Deal

You might be tempted to look for a discount fee by visiting a "low-fee clinic." I strongly advise against it. High-volume, low-fee veterinary clinics move so fast and furiously that they sometimes miss important problems. You won't get what you don't pay for.

Going forward, it appears that there will be fewer of these clinics. Pet owners are getting more savvy. They research their pet's diseases on the internet. Heck, some even read books like this one. Veterinarians are increasingly aware of their liability, too.

Our job is to advocate for the pet's needs at the start of the problem. But as technology and medicine advance, so do the costs. Not only do we have increasing equipment needs, but we must also hire and retain skilled and committed staff. None of that comes cheap. A good veterinarian will diagnose first and treat second. We don't look for ways to save our client's money by "trying this or that first and if it doesn't work we'll work on getting a diagnosis." You want a doctor who will go after the cause of the problem right from the start.

Index

ABOUT THE AUTHOR

Jeff Nichol, D.V.M., born in Detroit, Michigan, has been practicing full-time companion pet medicine and surgery since graduation from the College of Veterinary Medicine at Michigan State University in 1974. Dr. Nichol is a member of the American Veterinary Medical Association, the New Mexico Veterinary Medical Association, and has served as president of the Albuquerque Veterinary Association.

Dr. Nichol began practice in Albuquerque, NM and in 1976 moved to Sacramento, CA to practice and take additional training in cardiology. In 1978 he purchased the Adobe Animal Medical Center in Albuquerque and remains its hospital director. Adobe enjoys a four-year certification from the American Animal Hospital Association and is now a member hospital of National PetCare Centers.

The questions and answers that comprise a major portion of this book have been a popular weekly feature of the *Albuquerque Journal* since 1996. Dr. Nichol lives a charmed life in Albuquerque with his wife, Carolyn, and sons, Jake and Frank, along with family pets Peter Rabbit and Raoul.